MAKING ARBORS & TRELLISES

MAKING ARBORS & TRELLISES

25 Practical & Decorative Projects for Your Garden

MARCIANNE MILLER & OLIVIER ROLLIN

LARK BOOKS

A Division of Sterling Publishing Co., Inc.
New York

Dedication

To the writer/woodworkers of
David and Liliane Vowell's
Saturday Lunch Bunch in
Studio City, California, especially
Kazu Yamamoto and Richard Oliver.

—*Marcianne Miller*

To John and Anne Quigley of
Asheville, North Carolina, whose
amazement at seeing my name as co-author
of this book will be exceeded only by the
continuous warmth of their friendship.

—*Olivier Rollin*

Technical Editor: ANDY RAE
Art Director: CELIA NARANJO
Ilustrations: OLIVIER ROLLIN
Cover Design: BARBARA ZARETSKY
Photography: EVAN BRACKEN
Assistant Editor:
VERONIKA ALICE GUNTER
Editorial Assistance:
DANA LADE
RAIN NEWCOMB
Editorial Interns:
ANNE WOLFF HOLLYFIELD
NATHALIE MORNU
Production Assistant:
HANNES CHAREN
Production Intern:
SHANNON YOKELEY

SPECIAL PHOTOGRAPHY:
Antique Rose Emporium, pp. 36, 54-59,
   81, 93 (left)
Evan Bracken, pp. 30, 48, 95, 98, 105,
   108, 126, 136, 141
Diane Leis Dietrich, p. 92
Dick Dietrich, front cover, p. 84
Robin Dyer, p. 10
Derek Fell, pp. 7, 12, 18, 43, 79, 83,
   109
Richard Hasselberg. pp. 47, 75, 106
Horticultural Photography, p. 41
Dency Kane, p. 35
Charles Mann, pp. 8, 39
Sandra Stambaugh, pp. 121, 123
Mark Turner, pp. 20, 61, 101, 118, 128,
   132, 135, back cover (left)
Deidra Walpole, pp. 11, 16, 27, 29, 65,
   66, 70, 73, 115, back cover (right)

Library of Congress Cataloging-in-Publication Data Available

Miller Marcianne.
   Making arbors & trellises : 25 practical & decorative projects for
your garden / by Marcianne Miller and Olivier Rollin.
      p. cm.
   ISBN 1-57990-436-x (pbk.) 1-57990-296-0 (hb.)
   1. Arbors--Design and construction. 2. Trellises--Design and construction. I. Title: Making arbors and trellises. II. Rollin, Olivier. III. Title.

SB463.5 .M56 2002
684.1'8--dc21

                                          2001050498

10 9 8 7 6 5 4 3 2 1

Published by Lark Books, a division of
Sterling Publishing Co., Inc.
387 Park Avenue South, New York, N.Y. 10016

First Paperback Edition 2003
© 2002, Lark Books

Distributed in Canada by Sterling Publishing,
c/o Canadian Manda Group, One Atlantic Ave., Suite 105
Toronto, Ontario, Canada M6K 3E7

Distributed in the U.K. by:
Guild of Master Craftsman Publications Ltd.
Castle Place, 166 High Street Lewes East Sussex, England BN7 1XU
Tel: (+ 44) 1273 477374 Fax: (+ 44) 1273 478606
Email: pubs@thegmcgroup.com, Web: www.gmcpublications.com

Distributed in Australia by Capricorn Link (Australia) Pty Ltd.,
P.O. Box 704, Windsor, NSW 2756 Australia

If you have questions or comments about this book, please contact:
Lark Books
67 Broadway
Asheville, NC 28801
(828) 253-0467

Printed in China

ISBN 1-57990-436-x (pbk.) 1-57990-296-0 (hb.)

CONTENTS

Introduction

WHAT DO YOU DO WHEN YOUR spacious backyard could be the envy of your neighbors, but it's flat as a pancake and just as boring? Or you've run out of bare earth and you absolutely must have a harvest of fresh vegetables this year, as well as a new way to show off your favorite flowers? The solution is to grow *up*—and embrace the exciting possibilities of vertical landscaping with arbors and trellises. In *Making Arbors & Trellises* you'll learn how to build garden structures that are both beautiful and utilitarian and at the same time expand your growing universe from ground covers and hedges, to include vines, glorious vines.

From simple pole trellises in the cook's garden to "Oh, my gosh, that's gorgeous!" rose-covered arbors and elegant arched gateways, vertical landscaping structures are objects of purposeful intention. By their very presence, they announce, "this garden intends to stay around for a while." In the pages ahead, you'll find a wide range of projects, suitable for all kinds of gardens, that you'll be proud to make and display. The projects offer the chance to learn valuable construction techniques, such as shaping green wood, working with lattice, using templates, and making arcs—skills you can apply to many other projects, both indoors and outdoors.

There's an intriguing challenge to planning, making, decorating, and maintaining arbors and trellises because the process combines several skills. You are a gardener *and* a designer for you work with a trowel and a saw. You need to be precise in your construction, yet allow for the unpredictability of nature and how it affects the way plants will embellish your creation. This element of surprise makes building arbors and trellises exciting.

Making Arbors & Trellises is a collection of projects made from wood. To keep things simple yet interesting, we've divided the projects into those made from standard-dimension lumber (the kind you'll find readily at your local lumberyard or home center) and rustic materials, such as logs, branches, saplings, and bamboo.

Writing this book was an adventure for us—testing theories, revising designs, consulting with experts, learning about weather and plants, and exploring the nature of wood and how it stands the test of time. We hope you have as much pleasure reading the book and making the beautiful projects as we did presenting them to you.

Arbors create vertical landscaping and transform the look of any garden.

ARBOR AND TRELLIS BASICS

Some trellises, such as the Traditional Fan Trellis, can be completed in one weekend.

How to Use This Book

SEVERAL OF THE PROJECTS in this book are suitable for beginning woodworkers with a free weekend, but most require more time, and a few are downright ambitious. If you've never before built an outdoor garden structure, starting with arbors or trellises is a good idea. They require processes that may be repetitive, such as making lattice screens, and the more sophisticated projects can be time-consuming, but the projects don't require advanced woodworking techniques or a big outlay of equipment.

Regardless of your experience, you can get more out of this book if you follow a few tips. Read this basics section in its entirety so you can see the flow of the whole trellis/arbor building process. For weekend woodworkers especially, it's important to realize that making an arbor is a lot more than just making a bigger woodworking project. Budgeting your time properly among the various tasks of planning, production, and planting is the key to success.

We selected 25 classic arbors and trellises that demonstrate a variety of styles, materials, and assembly approaches, and we've pictured them in beautiful garden settings. Then, we adapted some of the designs to simplify their construction and account for the availability of materials. In these cases, your completed project will reflect the measurements and assembly information shown in the large construction drawings. All of the projects are accompanied by thorough step-by-step instructions.

You'll find a mix of standard-lumber and rustic wood projects, with the easier projects—the trellises—placed before the arbors for each category. The projects range in difficulty from "Hey, even I can do that!" to ones that will be the highlights of the local garden tour. With the weekend woodworker in mind, we adapted many of the designs to simplify them.

To determine whether you want to make a particular project, read through the instructions carefully, weighing your experience with the level of skill required. Gather all your tools and materials ahead of time. Everything you'll need is listed in the project instructions, with references to this basics section for more detailed information as needed. In addition, you'll find important safety reminders, and lots of tips we wish somebody had told us before we learned the hard way!

The Cutting List specified for each project gives you a great deal of information. It indicates the code numbers of the pieces, which are matched to the illustrations for easy reference. The "qty." (quantity) column indicates how many pieces you'll need to cut. The dimensions list indicates the exact cutting dimensions. The column, "Cut from" can be used as your shopping list since it indicates the amount and size of standard dimension lumber that you'll need to buy or rustic pieces to gather.

Lumber dimensions are listed in the usual way: thickness, width, length—and in inches. If you're using hardwood, which is sold by linear foot rather than in standard pre-cut lengths, just use the lengths in the Cutting List to help you calculate your hardwood needs. For rustic projects, the Gathering List indicates the diameter and length of the pieces (such as branches) you need to collect.

Many of the projects in the book have detailed illustrations. You have our permission to duplicate the illustrations in the book (for your own use, of course, not for commercial purposes) and keep them handy in your workspace so that you can look at them frequently.

By the very nature of most outdoor building projects, helpers are needed. Especially when you are gathering rustic materials, making measurements over a distance, lifting, carrying, holding and adjusting heavy pieces of lumber, or digging holes. In the project instructions, we suggest when you should "call in your helpers," but your own good common sense will be your real guide. Except in the woodshop, when it's often best to work without distraction, err on the side of more help rather than less.

Safety: First and Foremost Always

THE USUAL WOODWORKING SAFETY RULES apply to all the lumber projects. Use caution with all power tools, provide adequate ventilation, and work under good lighting. Wear safety glasses; the best are the wraparound ones which protect both the front and sides of your eyes, made with high-impact polycarbonate lenses. And remember your ears: power tools can cause permanent hearing damage, so use earplugs or hearing muffs when firing up a loud tool. You might consider a "no visitors" rule for children, pets, and others while you're working.

Always use a dust mask to avoid inhaling dust and other particulates when cutting and sanding wood. When working with pressure treated wood, you need more protection. Use a professional quality cartridge-type respirator, or a less expensive disposable respirator. Either choice should be equipped with a HEPA (High Efficiency Particulate Air) filter.

Dress properly for safety and make sure your helpers do, too. That means protective leather gloves and sturdy shoes or boots to protect feet from a wayward arbor post. (Metal-toed boots offer even more protection.) Even in the summertime, gathering materials and carrying lumber is safer when wearing long sleeves and long pants.

Remember Gathering Rule #1: Gathering always takes longer than you think it will. So wear protective clothing and footwear, and use sunscreen and insect repellent. Be sure to carry snacks and plenty of water. Keep an eye out for wildlife, including snakes, insects, spiders, and whoever else might not welcome your foraging activities.

Last, but not least, a word to those whose weekends are so precious they try to cram too much into them, exercising speed instead of caution, and risking injury. *Take your time.* One of the nice things about arbors and trellises is that it takes time for plants to grow on them. The plants don't feel rushed to finish their job. Why should you?

Lots of sun, a little rain—it doesn't take much to turn simple poles into beautiful garden accents.

Choosing Your Project

THE EASIEST VERTICAL LANDSCAPING project is a trellis. Basically a trellis is a structure made more or less from vertical supports and a lot of lattice, or similar pieces that crisscross each other in various ways.

Beginning vertical landscapers love trellises because they don't have to think much about them. Most trellises are utilitarian structures and as such they're pretty forgiving of beginner's mistakes. Disguise any imperfections with a fast-growing plant and nobody but your nosy woodworking buddies will be any wiser. Rustic trellises don't even require precise cutting, so they're ideal as first projects, especially when your helpers are young people.

Many trellises can simply be attached to something that's already there—walls, fences, and chimneys are the most logical supports. But anything whimsical will do, too, such as that old swingset the kids outgrew, or outdoor lampposts, or mailboxes. Let your imagination soar to its vertical limit!

Other trellises are freestanding. They range from the thrown-together pole tipis you see everywhere to carefully designed projects that can be transported to any spot in the yard, such as the Sun-Topped Pyramid Trellis on page 34.

Arbors are another story. Essentially they're trellises with a roof, but building one is a lot more than, "Hey, great photo, nice flowers, let's do it!" As bigger, more substantial, more permanent structures, arbors mean a greater invest-

Pole trellises make ideal rustic projects for beginners.

ment of time and money, and stability and solid construction are essential. Proper planning is crucial.

PROJECT PLANNING CHECKLIST

So many wonderful projects—how can you choose just one? Here's a simple checklist of factors to consider before committing your time and resources.

Site: Decide where to put your structure so it performs the function you want it to. Do you want it to be a delightful surprise for visitors as they come around the bend in the path, or do you want it in full view, covering an entire wall to keep your house cool in the summer? Will it get enough daylight for sun-loving plants? Be protected so winds won't blow it over? Be placed where you can observe its beauty from a window if you want, or at a distance to create a private

This screen has several benefits. It creates privacy and shade, frames a view, and allows breezes to pass through.

want, or at a distance to create a private get-away? *Scale:* Will your structure fit the amount of space you have? A small garden can't handle more than one arbor, but it might be able to have several trellises. You can place several arbors in a big garden, and you might want to group them for dramatic effect, such as the trio of Royal Blue Arches on page 65. Or each structure can serve a different function in its own location, such as the Grand Gateway on page 72, which marks a transition between sections of the garden, or the Lasting Legacy Arbor that (page 78) frames a view.

Style: Your Georgian hilltop manor needs outdoor structures of equal elegance. But in a cottage garden, a rustic piece might be a better choice. In a large garden you can mix styles, giving each garden "room" a different look. In a smaller garden, consistency of style is a better approach.

Schedule: When will you have enough time to build the structure? And dig the required holes? And round up helpers to assist you? Remember to plan for the time it takes to prune vining plants, train them to climb, and nourish them every year.

Saving the Structure: What kinds of wood preservative, stains, or paints will you use? And will you have time in the future for annual maintenance? (See Finishing Your Strutcure, page 29.)

Selection of Plants: You'll want to consider fragrance, color, growth pattern, and the kinds of wildlife that specific plants attract. If you want butterflies, that's fine. But who wants to sit under a fruit-bearing plant that attracts birds and their droppings, or bees and their stings? Save your trellises for attracting wildlife, and plant fragrant flowers on your arbors to attract humans. (See Choosing the Plants, page 32.)

Lumber Projects

ALTHOUGH EARLY ARBORS were made of brick and stone, wood has become the most popular material for arbors today, probably because wood projects are easier to make. Can you use any kind of wood for your outdoor structure? Well, you could, but left untreated, many woods deteriorate within three to five years when used outside and some won't last even that long. When you're considering outdoor standard lumber structures, your choices fall into two categories: wood that is naturally decay-resistant, and lumber that has been treated with chemical preservatives.

NATURALLY DECAY-RESISTANT WOOD

Naturally decay-resistant woods are wonderful woods. They last outdoors a long time, and take finishes easily without much preparation. In the best possible world, we'd love to use these woods to build outdoor structures. But due to many factors, including our dwindling forests, these desirable woods are becoming less available and more expensive. Following is a list of some natural woods suitable for outdoor structures.

White or yellow cedar: Durable and resistant to moisture and fungal decay. Can be treated to resist insects. Weathers and finishes nicely. Readily available.

Redwood: Naturally decay and termite-resistant. Beautiful texture and color when weathered. Expensive.

Cypress: Highly resistant to insects and moisture decay. Easy to work. Wear gloves and pre-drill for fasteners to avoid splintering.

White oak: Hard and durable. Difficult to obtain in thicknesses of more than 1".

Black or yellow locust: Extremely decay-resistant, making it a good choice for ground posts. Very hard, so make sure cutting tools are sharp. Can be difficult to find.

South American mahogany: Resistant to decay and easily worked. Weathers well. Very expensive.

If you decide to use a naturally decay-resistant wood for your project, look for air-dried or kiln-dried stock. Be aware that even dried wood, when used outdoors and subject to sunlight, rain, and changes in temperature, will swell and shrink. To minimize these effects, treat your outdoor projects with water repellent or wood-stabilizing finishes. (See Finishing Your Structure, page 29.)

PRESSURE TREATED WOOD

Because of the cost and frequent unavailability of natural wood, the alternative for most outdoor garden projects is less expensive pressure treated (PT) wood. We designed most of our standard lumber projects with this wood in mind.

PT wood (usually southern yellow pine or Douglas fir) is treated with water that forces preservatives into its pores, forming a thin sheet of concentrated preservative on the exterior of the lumber surrounding the core. The type of preservative, the amount retained in the wood, and the depth of its penetration vary.

The most common wood preservative for home use is chromated copper arsenate (CCA). Preservatives don't make the wood waterproof; they just make the wood unappetizing as food for the

---

LUMBER: THE REAL DIMENSIONS

As you probably know, lumber is cut at the mill in standard sizes. These are its nominal dimensions. A 2 x 4 is indeed 2" thick x 4" wide when it travels to the mill. When it leaves the mill, however, that same 2 x 4 emerges with an actual dimension of 1½" x 3½" due to drying and milling procedures. The milling process doesn't affect the length. Each lumber project in the book lists the actual dimensions after cutting in the "dimensions" column in the cutting list. The nominal dimensions are in the "cut from" column.

organisms that like to feed on it. As long as the shell of preservative stays intact, the core is protected.

PT wood comes in two grades, which are clearly indicated: *above ground* and *below ground*. Of course, choose the below ground grade for the posts of your projects.

The chemicals forced into the wood during the process are more prominent near the skin, or outside surface, of the lumber. Thus, when you cut the lumber you expose the less-treated core to the elements. The solution is to treat any cut surfaces—especially end grain areas—with more preservative, which you can buy in small cans where you get your PT wood.

Some precautions when working with PT wood are in order. Always work with the material in a well-ventilated area, preferably outdoors. When cutting or sanding, use a respirator with a HEPA filter to protect you from the chemical-laden dust. Just like plywood and other wood products that are glued or impregnated with chemical solutions, PT wood should not be burned. Dispose of PT wood and sawdust in appropriate landfills.

Use leather gloves to avoid a possible reaction to the preservative. Wash your hands before eating, and clean and sanitize any scratches or cuts you might receive when working with the wood. Wash the clothes you wear when working with PT wood separately from other laundry, then dry them on a line outside, if possible. Since research on PT wood is always being updated, you should look for specific safety and handling information from the consumer tip sheet available where you buy your lumber.

Once it is exposed to the elements, PT wood takes about a year to fully season. This means you shouldn't paint or stain your project for a year. If you get impatient and do apply a finish, you'll be wasting time and money, because whatever you put on unseasoned PT wood will just bubble and peel off. It's better to wait.

COMPOSITE WOOD: SUITABLE FOR ARBORS AND TRELLISES?

There's a rapidly growing interest in composite lumber that is chemical-free and also decay-resistant. This composite is made from recycled plastic, such as grocery bags, and wood waste. It is most commonly used to build decks and can be found through dealers and some lumberyards. You can make arbors and trellises from this product if you're aware of several caveats. Although the composite lumber can be cut, fastened, and even painted in ways similar to techniques used for PT wood, composite wood is flexible, due to the plastic ingredients. Thus it can't handle a lot of weight. If used as a crossbeam, a piece of composite lumber would need to be supported every 16 or 20" or so, depending on its size and length, therefore the design would need to incorporate these needs. Also, it might be difficult to find composite wood in the sizes indicated in a project's cutting list. If you want to try adapting a project to use composite wood, make sure you follow the manufacturer's instructions (not all composite products are the same). And start small with a simple trellis or arbor.

TOOLS

Most of the tools you need to construct your standard lumber projects might already be in a toolbox kicking around your house. If not, see the list below—we've put together a tool kit of essential tools. One tool, a trammel, you can easily make yourself. (See Making and Using a Trammel on page 16.) If additional tools are needed for a particular project, we list them in the project's tool list, according to size, with the smallest ones listed first. It's a good idea to gather the smaller tools in one toolbox so you can easily carry them to the work site, and can keep them together once you're there.

BASIC TOOL KIT
- Carpenter's pencil
- Felt-tip marker
- Chalk
- 16' tape measure
- Utility knife
- $1/2$"-1" bevel-edge chisel
- Wood rasp
- 100-grit sandpaper
- String
- C-clamps, 6" long
- Pipe clamps, 24" long
- 6" pencil compass or string compass (see page 16)
- Trammel (see page 16)
- 45/90° plastic drafting triangle (available at art supply stores)
- 12" combination square
- Framing square
- 20 oz. claw hammer
- Nail set
- Pliers
- Ratchet and socket set, or a set of box wrenches
- Coping saw with fine blade

HOW ECO-FRIENDLY IS PT WOOD?

Like other modern conveniences, it's a mixed bag. Yes, it contains toxic preservatives in order to do its job, and although the amount of chemicals that leach out of the wood is considered by many experts to be extremely minimal, some organic gardeners won't use PT wood to make raised beds for vegetables. However, since it lasts such a long time, PT wood is the first wood of choice for parks, wildlife sanctuaries, and recreation areas around the world. By using PT wood, we can reduce logging, and allow other, more valuable lumber to reach full growth. Recent good news: Pressure treated wood that uses a new arsenic-free preservative called ACQ is becoming more available. Ask about it at your local lumberyard.

- Crosscutting handsaw
- Line level
- 4' carpenter's level
- 8' straightedge (any straight piece of lumber; plywood is fine)
- Power drill with assortment of drill bits and a driver bit (see Hardware, page 16)
- Pair of saw horses
- 6' stepladder

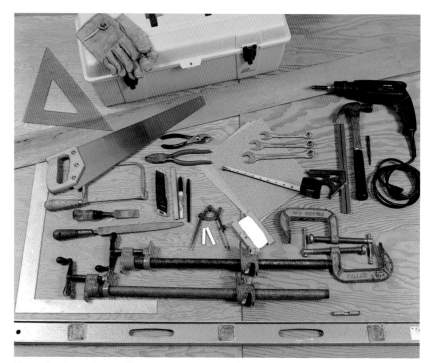

These basic tools + safety masks and filters (page 14) = your Basic Tool Kit.

MAKING AND USING A TRAMMEL

Arcs are essential parts of the design of many arbors. Making them is easy.

Several of the projects in this book require that you draw an arc. While you can make small arcs with a regular pencil compass or a length of string tied to a pencil (called a *string compass*), larger pieces, such as the arcs for the Royal Blue Arches project on page 65, are too big for a normal compass. That's when you'll need a trammel, and it's easy to make one yourself.

A *trammel* consists of a length of wood with a screw at one end and a pencil at the other end. (See fig. 1.) The distance from the screw to the pencil equals the desired radius. By pivoting the trammel around the tip of the screw, you can draw arcs of practically any size. Plus, you won't have to deal with any stretching or tangling as can happen with a string compass.

To make a trammel, select a straight piece of wood about 1/2" thick by 2" wide and a few inches longer than your longest desired radius. Drive a screw into one end, allowing the tip of the screw to protrude about 1/4" from the back. Then measure the desired radius from the tip of the screw, and make a notch at that distance for a carpenter's pencil with a handsaw. (We prefer using a carpenter's pencil rather than a small-leaded regular pencil, which wears quickly and breaks easily.) A 1/8" saw kerf is sufficient to hold the pencil in the trammel, as shown in the detail in figure 1. If you need to make concentric arcs, such as for an arch, simply cut another notch for the second radius.

HARDWARE

In air-dried wood, screws provide greater holding power than nails. For that reason our instructions usually indicate the use of screws, especially with arbor proj-

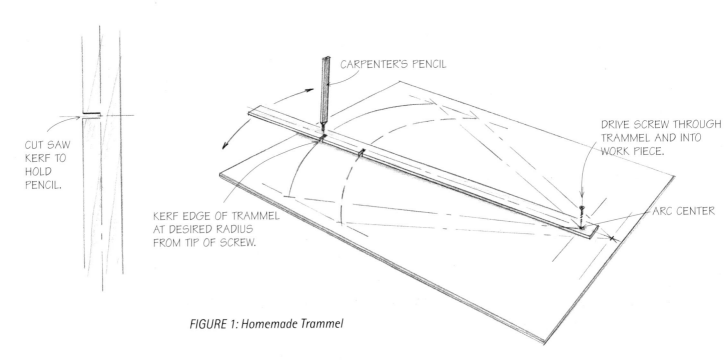

CUT SAW KERF TO HOLD PENCIL.

CARPENTER'S PENCIL

DRIVE SCREW THROUGH TRAMMEL AND INTO WORK PIECE.

KERF EDGE OF TRAMMEL AT DESIRED RADIUS FROM TIP OF SCREW.

ARC CENTER

FIGURE 1: Homemade Trammel

ects. But nails are often handier and more efficient for assembling rustic structures, where screws would be harder to install and more obtrusive in the finished design.

SCREWS

Purists love stainless steel screws for their long-lasting durability. Use them if your budget allows. But for most of us, deck screws are a less-expensive choice for outdoor wood projects. These screws are specially coated to resist the weather's effects, especially rust. You can drive deck screws with a Phillips screwdriver, but for maximum power with very little fuss we recommend fitting an electric drill with a Phillips screwdriver bit, called a *driver bit*. With this setup you can drive screws all day long without having your arms or wrists give out. For the best look, drive screws flush with or slightly below the surface of the wood, a process called *countersinking*.

When you need extra holding power, use a lag bolt. Lag bolts (also called lags screws) are essentially bolts with a modified wood-screw thread, used typically in projects that involve large timbers.

NAILS

Most nails in rustic projects are finish nails, which have a smooth steel shank and a small, tapered head that conceals itself well when driven into wood. Cement-coated nails are excellent for use in rustic projects. Their coating allows them to hold up to the stresses from drying and shrinking that occur in green lumber, and they resist rusting. Some people like to use common steel nails in rustic projects because they rust to a nice color, but rust they do, so weigh looks against the shorter life rusty nails will bring to the structure.

DRILLING PILOT HOLES

For most projects, you'll drill pilot holes before driving a screw or nail. This allows you to drive a fastener more easily, and also prevents the wood from splitting, especially near the ends of boards. Pilot holes should go through both of the pieces you're assembling, but not quite as deep as the length of the screw or nail you'll be using. Size your pilot holes to the diameter of your screw's shank—not to the larger diameter of its threads. This way the threads will grip the wood. Below are the sizes of pilot bits that match specific screws or nails used in the projects in this book.

DRILL BIT SIZE FOR DRILLING PILOT HOLES	NAIL/SCREW SIZE
$1/16$"	4d and 6d nails
$3/32$"	8d nails
$1/8$"	10d nails
$3/32$"	$1/2$, $3/4$, 1, $1 1/4$, 2, and $2 1/2$" screws
$1/8$"	3, $3 1/2$ and 4" screws
$1/4$"	$3/8$" lag screws

CONCEALING YOUR HARDWARE

If you want a smooth, unblemished surface on your project—a good idea if you're going to use paint—you have a couple options for hiding screws or nails. The easiest method is to make sure the fasteners are countersunk well, then fill the holes with wood putty. The putty not only hides the fasteners, but protects them as well. Another option for concealing the head of a screw is to first use a regular drill bit to drill a counterbored hole about ½" deep and slightly bigger than the diameter of the screw's head. Then drill a pilot hole through the counterbore and drive the screw. Once you've installed all the screws, glue short lengths of dowel stock into the counterbored holes and over the head of the screws. When the glue has dried, saw or chisel any protruding dowels flush with the surface. One tip: Tackle your hole-filling chores during construction rather than the finishing stage. It's tedious work, and better done now than later.

Three templates are used in the Conversation Arbor.

SPECIAL TECHNIQUES

There are a number of special construction techniques mentioned throughout the book, and they're worth getting to know. Not only will they make the process of building a specific project easier, but learning these techniques will also expand your construction skills for other projects.

USING TEMPLATES

Several projects show illustrations that contain a template or two, which are designed to help with shaping curved or complex parts. The instructions usually indicate to enlarge the template to full size. Here's how to do it: On a piece of posterboard, draw a grid of 1" squares with a pencil and ruler, using the same number of squares that you see on the illustration. Then re-draw the shape of the piece on your grid freehand, working one square at a time. You don't have to be an artist to make a successful enlargement. Once you've drawn the shape, cut along your outlines and use the posterboard template to trace the actual shape onto the piece stock. Or you can simply enlarge the templates on a photocopier.

CUTTING DADOES

Many of the project instructions call for making one or more dadoes. A dado is a slot or groove cut into the edge of a piece of lumber. Dadoes are a simple way to join two pieces at right angles and to give a joint strength.

As shown in figure 2, first measure and lay out the dado on your stock. Depending on the type of dado needed, you can often use the adjoining piece to help with laying out the joint by placing it directly on the stock and tracing its width. Once you've laid out the joint, make a series of closely spaced cuts across the grain of the wood, using a handsaw. Remove the bulk of the waste by chopping across the grain with a sharp chisel and a hammer, then smooth the bottom by hand with light paring cuts from the chisel. If you need to adjust the width of a dado, use the chisel again to make small chopping cuts until the joint fits perfectly.

TOENAILING

Toenailing refers to the process of driving nails or screws at an angle into the side of a piece of lumber to attach it to another piece of lumber. You'll need to use this technique when a piece of lumber is so thick or wide that you can't drive a fastener through it, or when angling a screw or nail through the first piece is the only way to gain access. The process of toenailing is simple, as shown in figure 3: Hold a drill bit at roughly

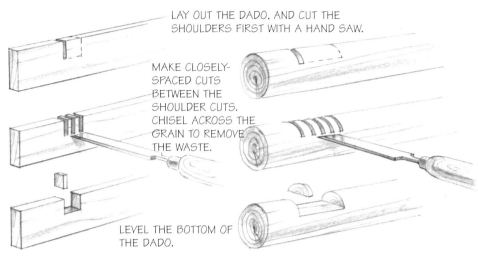

LAY OUT THE DADO, AND CUT THE SHOULDERS FIRST WITH A HAND SAW.

MAKE CLOSELY-SPACED CUTS BETWEEN THE SHOULDER CUTS. CHISEL ACROSS THE GRAIN TO REMOVE THE WASTE.

LEVEL THE BOTTOM OF THE DADO.

FIGURE 2: Making Dado Cuts

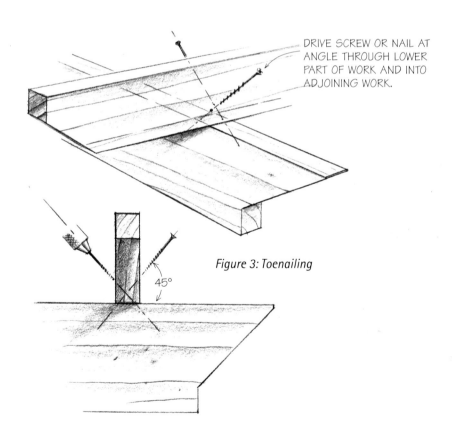

DRIVE SCREW OR NAIL AT ANGLE THROUGH LOWER PART OF WORK AND INTO ADJOINING WORK.

Figure 3: Toenailing

45°

45° to the work to drill a pilot hole for the nail or screw. Then follow this same angle as you install the fastener.

Rustic Projects

RUSTIC STRUCTURES are made from branches and saplings that are bent and nailed into shape. Because the materials are unmilled and often covered with bark, rustic projects have a wildness that works beautifully in cottage gardens or for landscaping with an eclectic style. Because imperfections are part of their charm, rustic trellises are great projects for children to help with, or for the once-in-a-blue-moon weekend worker.

Green wood, cut no more than 24 hours before, is supple and easy to bend into different shapes.

TYPES OF WOOD

What's the best kind of wood for rustic projects? Often it's whatever kind of wood you like, and what's available. If you can find dried logs of decay-free wood, by all means go for it. One of the most flexible types of wood is willow, and it's a good choice for a beginner, particularly if you have young helpers. Bamboo is a marvelously sturdy and adaptable material that is naturally weather-resistant and can be left unfinished. If you haven't worked with bamboo yet, try the bamboo projects on pages 117 and 120, and 123 and you'll be a convert. If you don't have access to a grove of bamboo where you can gather it freely, look for bamboo in garden supply stores and on the internet.

The rustic projects call for both dried and "green" branches and saplings. "Green" refers to the high moisture content in the wood of a freshly cut sapling: the greener the wood, the more supple it will be when it comes time to bend or coax it into position. "Freshly cut" means the wood was cut no more than 24 hours ago. After that, the wood becomes more brittle and prone to snapping or cracking as you work it.

Dried material means just that: it's dry, hard, and not supple at all. This can be a useful attribute if rigidity is needed, such as for the main frame or posts for an arbor. Freshly cut wood dries naturally at the rate of about an inch of thickness a year. That means if a project calls for a dried branch that is 1½" in diameter, it would have been cut and left to dry in a protected area for at least 18 months. Avoid wood that has fallen on the ground because it might carry hordes of visiting insects and fungi, both of which are detrimental to the wood, and almost impossible to get rid of. And don't scavenge in long-standing wood-piles either, for the same reasons.

GATHERING RUSTIC MATERIALS

Where can you find rustic materials? Anywhere you can get permission—private property, or land belonging to logging companies and recreation areas. Make friends of tree surgeons, highway teams, real estate developers, and anyone you see cutting down a tree. Whatever your source, always ask permission to enter the property and remove materials.

The main goal when gathering your materials is to look for the approximate diameter and length called for in the project. If a project calls for a curved piece or two, use your keen eyesight to search for the appropriate sweep among the many shapes that nature provides. You'll get better at locating the right shapes and sizes by foraging through the woods.

RUSTIC TOOL KIT

For gathering and building rustic projects, you'll need to add a few tools to the ones in the basic tool kit (see page 15). If you're a gardener, you probably already have most of them:

- Roll of tie wire (16 to 19 gauge)
- Bow saw
- Wire cutters
- Shears
- Pruners
- Loppers

These gathering tools + basic tool kit (page 15) = your Rustic Tool Kit.

PROLONGING THE LIFE OF RUSTIC STRUCTURES

By their nature, rustic projects are not as long-lived as lumber projects, so be forewarned. Leaving the bark on the poles looks wonderfully charming, but be aware the bark also provides a hideaway for bugs and other destructive organisms. You can prolong the life of a rustic structure by stripping the bark off the bases of the posts and dipping them in a preservative before you put them into the ground. Also, rustic arches don't support the weight of heavy climbers such as wisteria and rambling roses. Choose lightweight climbers such as morning glories and clematis.

Installing Your Project

MANY OF THE SIMPLER PROJECTS in this book, especially the rustic projects and several trellises, can merely be placed on the ground. But the more complex arbors and trellises need careful site preparation, layout measurements, and posthole digging. It's essential that you plan enough time for these tasks. Above all, you want to dig the holes in the correct manner. Doing it properly the first time means you won't have to deal with the difficult task of making major adjustments to the arbor during installation. Assemble a kit of tools that will help you prepare the site and dig the holes, as shown in the photo below.

Digging and measuring tools + batterboards (page 22) = your Digging Kit.

THE DIGGING KIT

Whether you're digging four holes or 40, you'll need the same tools—a combination of measuring tools and digging tools, some of which are also in the Basic Tool Kit (page 15).

- Marking pen
- 16' tape measure
- Framing square
- Mason's string: For holding a line level. Instead of the more popular nylon, get the old-fashioned white cotton string if you can because it won't stretch.
- Line level: Good for measuring long lengths for level. A small bubble vial encased in a metal or plastic tube that hooks over a length of string. When you pull the string taut horizontally and the bubble in the vial is centered, the line is level.
- 4' carpenter's level
- 8'-long straightedge: Combined with a carpenter's level for measuring level over 8' distances or less. Find a board with two parallel and straight edges; a piece of plywood is an excellent candidate.
- Plumb bob: For finding plumb, or vertical with the ground. A cylindrical weight with a string at one end and a point tip at the other end. You hang the bob by the string so its tip is directly above the spot you're measuring.
- Small sledgehammer or 24 oz. claw hammer
- Hatchet or handsaw
- Batterboards (See information on batterboards on next page.)
- Metal rake

- Shovel
- Posthole digger, auger bit, or star drill: For digging postholes. Invest in a posthole digger with clamshell-style blades at least 9" long, which will work on most soils and remove as much dirt as possible without making the holes wider than they should be. If you're only doing one project, consider renting a posthole digger. Use an auger bit (manual or electric) if you're in sandy or soft soil. If you encounter rocks, you'll need a star drill (manual or electric).
- Gravel: To line the bottom of postholes. For ordinary conditions, look for 3/4" "drainage grade" stones, a mix of stones from 1/2" to 1" in diameter. If in doubt, ask a local expert for advice on the choice of gravel. For small projects it's more convenient to buy by the sack instead of by the cubic foot.

PREPARING THE SITE

Preparing the site for your structure and digging postholes can be done at any stage of putting your project together. If you need to work around your helpers' schedules, do so. Or if you know that you really require a change of pace from woodworking, then sandwich the site preparation between your building sessions. But for most projects, it's best to tackle this prep work after your project has been assembled.

The first goal in site preparation is to make the ground surface flat. Use a shovel or rake to level and smooth the area. Clear at least 2' to 3' on either side of the perimeter so you'll have room to work, as shown in figure 5 on page 25. There may, of course, be slight variances in level. That's OK: You'll deal with more exacting tolerances later. For now, concentrate on getting the site as flat as possible by eye. Now is also the time to clear the pathway to the site so it's safe to travel when you and your helpers are carrying tools and heavy pieces of lumber.

Once the site is roughly leveled and cleared, mark out the approximate location of the postholes by referring to the project dimensions. Mark these spots with twigs stuck in the ground, or use marker flags, the small plastic flags used by contractors and surveyors.

LAYING OUT PRECISE POSTHOLE LOCATIONS WITH BATTERBOARDS

To find out exactly where to dig your postholes so they'll line up with the posts of your project, you'll need to use a system of *batterboards*, as shown in figure 4 on page 24. Batterboards help establish the exact centers of the postholes using a system of lines strung between them. You'll need a pair of batterboards for each corner of the site, which means that projects with four posts will require a total of eight batterboards.

Making batterboards is easy. Each batterboard consists of three parts, the crosspiece and two sharpened stakes, each made from 2 x 4s. (See fig. 4.) Measure and cut all the pieces ahead of time and bring them to the site. To construct eight batterboards, you'll need eight crosspieces and 16 stakes.

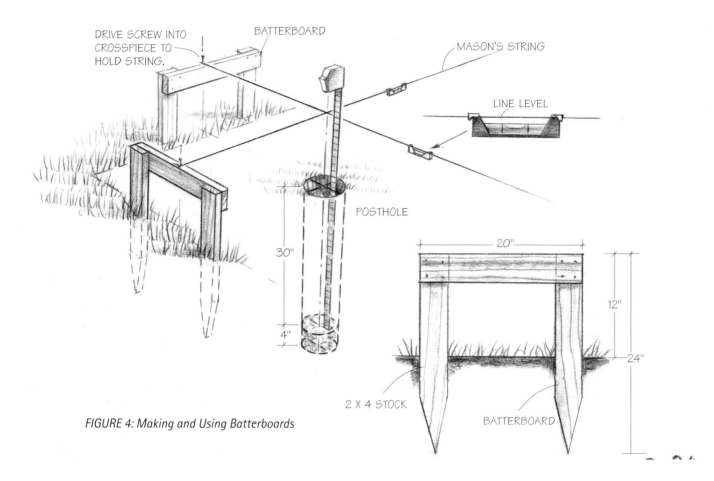

DRIVE SCREW INTO CROSSPIECE TO HOLD STRING.

BATTERBOARD

MASON'S STRING

LINE LEVEL

POSTHOLE

30"

4"

20"

12"

24"

2 X 4 STOCK

BATTERBOARD

FIGURE 4: *Making and Using Batterboards*

Crosspieces are usually 20" long and stakes are 24" long, sharpened at one end. Sharpen the end of each stake carefully with a handsaw or hatchet so that the point is centered, which will allow the stake to go straight into the earth when you install it. Attach the crosspieces at right angles to the stakes with 2½" screws. Since you'll be finished with the batterboards once you've dug the holes, consider disassembling them and recycling the pieces to make any temporary braces you might need in the project. (See Bracing Your Structure, page 28.)

Once you've assembled the batterboards, refer to figure 5 to lay out and position them around your site. Use a heavy hammer or a small sledgehammer to tap the batterboards into the ground, leaving about 1' above ground, as shown in figure 4. Drive screws into the tops of the batterboards, then attach lengths of mason's string to the screws and use a line level to level the batterboards to each other. If the distance between opposite batterboards is less than 8', you can use a straight piece of 2 x 4 in lieu of a line level and string. Bridge the 2 x 4 across the batterboards, placing a carpenter's level on top of the board to level the batterboards to each other. Follow the steps in figure 5 to mark the exact

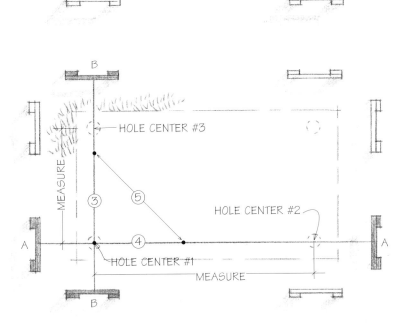

Part 1

1. Install all eight batterboards into the ground, 2' to 3' from the rough posthole locations. The tops of the batterboards should be approximately 12" above ground.

Part 2

2. Drive screws into the tops of opposite batterboards and stretch a line (A-A) between the screws, roughly centering the line over the posthole marks. Level the line by using a line level and adjusting the height of the batterboards.

3. Stretch a second line (B-B) between adjacent batterboards and roughly square to line A-A. Level line B-B so that it touches line A-A. Make a mark where the two lines intersect. This is the center of the first posthole.

4. Using the mathematical formula of 3/4/5, make a mark 4' from the first posthole center along line A-A. Then mark 3' from the same posthole center along line B-B. Measure the diagonal line (called the hypotenuse) between these two marks. Shift line B-B until the hypotenuse measures 5'. Your lines are now dead square to each other.

5. Referring to dimensions on the project illustrations, measure the first posthole center to mark the second and third posthole centers on lines A-A and B-B.

Part 3

6. Stretch two more lines (C-C and D-D) between the remaining batterboards, making them roughly square to each other.

7. Square lines C-C and D-D using the same 3/4/5 formula as indicated in step 4. Where the two lines intersect is the fourth posthole center.

8. Check that the layout of your postholes is square by comparing opposite diagonals, measuring from corner to corner. When the two measurements are equal, your layout is square

9. Suspend a plumb bob from each posthole center and mark the exact posthole center on the ground with marker flags.

center locations of the postholes with marker flags.

Once you've marked the posthole centers, you'll need to remove the lines temporarily to keep them out of the way during digging. To do this, untie only one end of each line, and leave all the screws in place. You'll need to reposition the lines later when checking the depth of the postholes

DIGGING POSTHOLES

Before you dig the holes for your posts, you'll need to consider a few things, such as what kind of soil you have, the diameter and depth of your postholes, and how cold the earth gets in the winter in your region.

For the projects in this book, we recommend the simple earth-and-gravel fill method: shovel in a 4" layer of gravel to cover the bottom of the posthole, position the post, then backfill with dirt. This method keeps water from collecting in the vicinity of the posts, and works fine in stable soils—not soil with high clay content (where slippage can occur) or in sandy earth. Many people prefer concrete post footings for more unstable soils, and will argue that concrete grants greater post longevity.

This is not necessarily the case for all locations. When in doubt, get advice from local experts to see if concrete has proved better in your specific area.

Sizing your holes correctly is important. As a general rule, postholes should be twice as wide as the width of the posts. For example, if a post is 4" wide, your hole should be 8" in diameter. Hole depth should be roughly one-third of the height of the post above ground, plus an additional 4" to handle a 4" layer of gravel below the post. Thus the holes specified in most of the arbor projects in this book are 34" deep (4" of gravel plus 30" of post below ground), as shown in figure 6.

Hole depth, however, can vary. For example, you'll need to dig deeper holes if the structure you're installing is particularly heavy or large, or if you're planning to attach a swing or other heavy item to the design (such as in the Stately Arbor on page 94). Another consideration is *frost heave*, the phenomenon that occurs when water in the soil freezes, which causes the soil to expand and "heave" and push or move anything buried in the earth—including your arbor posts. Well-drained soils don't hold water, so if you're lucky enough to have this type of soil you needn't be concerned about frost heave. And warmer southern climates won't experience the same degree of freezing found in colder, northern areas. If you're in doubt as to your local frost conditions and the type of soil you have, get advice from local experts.

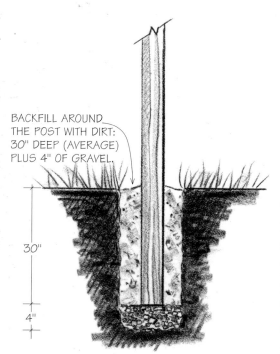

BACKFILL AROUND THE POST WITH DIRT: 30" DEEP (AVERAGE) PLUS 4" OF GRAVEL.

30"

4"

FIGURE 6: Posthole Anatomy

Your local building inspectors, contractors, and professional fence builders can advise you on how deep you must dig your postholes to prevent heaving. If you do need to modify the lengths of the posts in a given project, make sure to allow at least 7' of clearance between the ground and the underside of any overhead beams.

Once you're ready to dig the holes, use the marker flags as a guide and dig each hole straight down. Keep dirt piles some distance from the holes so passersby and pets don't accidentally push soil back into the holes. Once you've dug to the correct depth, shovel in 4" of gravel into the bottom of the hole, and use a spare 2 x 4 to tamp the gravel so it's level and firm.

Accurate hole depth is key to successful arbor installation. The four (or more) holes must all be precisely the same depth, or the arbor won't be level when you install it. To check hole depth, reposition the lines on your batterboards as you did when laying out the posthole centers so they intersect once again at the hole locations. Measure from two intersecting lines to the bottom of a hole with a tape measure, as shown in figure 4, page 24. This distance should be the same for all the holes. If necessary, adjust the depth of the holes by adding or removing gravel from the bottom of the holes. When you install the posts, remember to avoid knocking dirt into your carefully prepared holes.

Arbors mark the transition between different sections of a garden.

BRACING YOUR STRUCTURE

Once the structure (an arbor usually) is in the ground you may need to brace it temporarily to keep it stable before working on it further. The two types of temporary braces are *crossbraces* and *post ground braces*, which are illustrated in figure 7. Not all the projects need bracing. For the ones that do, we've indicated that in the materials list and the instructions.

Crossbraces hold the posts together so you can transport the assembly or install it into the ground. Make the crossbraces from 1 x 4' material about 8' long, and secure them with 2½" screws to the posts in a crossed pattern, as shown in figure 7. Be sure to drive a screw through both boards where they intersect in the center to further stiffen the assembly.

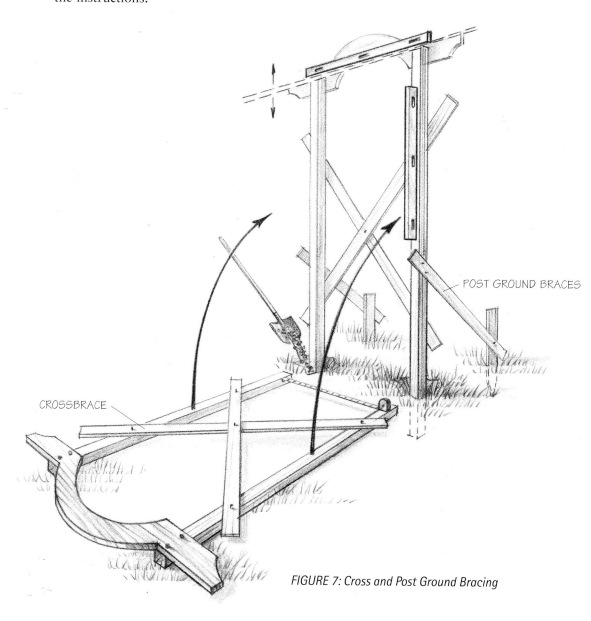

POST GROUND BRACES

CROSSBRACE

FIGURE 7: Cross and Post Ground Bracing

Once you've inserted the posts into the ground, post ground braces ensure the posts remain plumb and level while other pieces are being attached to them and before the final backfill of earth. Each post ground brace consists of 1 x 4 stock about 3' long screwed to a 2 x 4 stake roughly 2' long. Shape a point on one end of the stake with a hatchet, and hammer that end into the ground. Attach one end of the 1 x 4 about one-third up the post with a few 2½" screws. Then secure the opposite end to the stake with 2" screws, placing a level against a post to check that your structure is plumb. A typical arbor with four or more posts requires only two pairs of ground braces. To brace a single post that stands by itself, you'll need two ground braces on either side of the post. Be prepared to loosen braces to shift posts when adjusting the height of the arbor, or when re-checking for plumb during the final construction stage.

FINISHING YOUR STRUCTURE

In addition to your personal preference for color and type of finish, the final look of your structure depends mostly on the type of material from which it's made.

If you choose natural wood for your project (see Naturally Decay-Resistant Wood, page 13), you can apply the finish either before you assemble or immediately after installation, which is a gratifying way to achieve color right away. If you use pressure treated wood, you'll need to let the structure weather

for about a year, then you can stain or paint it to your heart's content.

There are three essential finishes for your outdoor lumber structures, and they vary in the amount of protection they offer from the destructive effects of sunlight, moisture, and fungi and other organisms, and by how much they affect the natural look of the wood. *Clear pen-*

Paint hides defects in woods and turns any arbor into an attention-getter.

etrating wood finishes, sometimes called *water inhibitors*, are colorless and do little to alter the natural look of the wood. Water inhibitors are used often on decks and railings to keep the elements at bay. They're quite convenient to use, since they penetrate the wood and can be applied to new wood without any preparation. The drawback to penetrating finishes is that they don't offer as much

protection as other finishes. Make sure you get a clear finish sealer and not a sanding sealer, which is a finish designed for use under other topcoats.

Exterior stains that are formulated for outdoor use allow you to add muted colors, and are ideal for applying to rough surfaces. Like clear penetrating finishes, stains soak into the wood, making it easy to get the color into nooks and crannies

Arbors with elegant, stately lines look best when painted.

of irregular surfaces. In addition to providing protection from the elements, stains are available in a wide range of colors, allowing you to color-coordinate all your outdoor structures with your house and overall landscaping design. Stains are also convenient to use. They don't need an undercoat, so you can apply them quickly. Stains are manufactured in both oil and water-based versions. Both work well, although the water-based variety is easier to handle and clean up. Lighter stains have a transparent appearance, showing more of the wood's imperfections, and they don't weather as well. Heavily colored stains are closer to paint in their coverage ability, containing more solids and lasting longer. But since stains penetrate the wood instead of forming a film, any defects in the wood will still show.

Paint, more costly and less convenient to use than stain, is best used on smooth surfaces. But paint can pay for itself by lasting longer than other finishes. And paint, unlike stain, conceals the imperfections in wood because it forms a film on the surface. You'll need to use a primer before applying a topcoat of paint. Paint primers penetrate the wood, giving the paint a surface to which it can bond, and making it easier to apply the topcoat of paint.

Like stains, paint comes in oil- and water-based formulas. Oil-based paints are expensive, troublesome to clean up, and need to be thinned with solvent, which can have vapors that are both toxic and flammable. However, oil paints are more effective than the water-based varieties, especially when applied to oily woods like cedar and redwood, because the oil in the paint prevents extractives in the wood from bleeding through. Paint comes in various gloss levels, from flat to semigloss to gloss. In general, the higher the gloss, the more durable the coating.

Keep in mind that any finish will require regular maintenance, which usually means recoating once a year or so to keep your project looking fresh. In this regard, paint is the most troublesome, since you'll have to sand the surface first to remove any peeling or chipping before applying a fresh coat. Penetrating finishes such as stains and water inhibitors need only a clean surface for recoating, so a quick scrub with a brush or nylon pad will suffice to prep the surface for a fresh application. It's a good idea to check the manufacturer's instructions first to get an idea of the maintenance schedule before deciding on which finish to use.

No finish at all is another option to consider. Yes—you can leave your project to weather naturally. Of course, your structure won't last as long—but eventually all outdoor wood projects will succumb to nature. However, you can relish the fact that no finish work is needed once you've built your structure, and you can also enjoy the natural look of weathered wood in its various hues and tones.

Choosing the Plants

What comes first, the structure—or the plants you want to grow on it? Yes! The relationship between vines and the arbors and trellises they climb is one of the closest partnerships in the garden.

In this section are some basic tips to help you select vining plants that will be right for your garden. Throughout the book, wherever space permitted, we decorated the pages with photos of plants suitable for the projects in the book.

Vining plants put all their energy into their foliage, leaving the vines weak, which is why they need support to climb. Some have stems that twine (such as jasmine and honeysuckle) which can't turn on a support as wide as an arbor post, but could do just fine on a narrow ribbed trellis. Plants with tendrils (special growths at the end of stems or leaves), such as grapes, reach out until they find something to hold onto, so they can grow on both vertical and horizontal surfaces. Other plants such as wintercreeper euonymus climb by aerial rootlets so you only have to help them in the beginning and then keep them pruned. Roses, by the way, are not natural climbers; thorns help them hook into supports, but they really need to be trained in order to climb up.

Vegetable or flower? Although veggies are usually relegated to trellises, you can add flowers like nasturtiums to the salad harvest of tomatoes, squash, beans, and peas, and everybody's happy. Arbors are more suitable for flowers, unless it's the fascinating hyacinth bean with its gorgeous purple pods.

Light or heavy? Delicate lattice structures need lightweight plants, such as morning glories. Large sturdy arbors can support heavy climbers, like rambling roses.

Fragrance? The pleasure that comes from garden fragrances is what inspires many people to build an arbor. The three superstars in the fragrance division are

See what we mean by not worrying someone will notice imperfections on your trellis? The vigorous lavender trumpet vine hides and beautifies any mistakes.

Lady Betty Balfour Clematis

roses, wisteria, and honeysuckle.

Fast or slow? Many of the most popular vining plants are fast-growers, annuals such as nasturtiums and morning glories, and perennial favorites, including clematis and the climbing hydrangea.

Green or bare? Most plants flower only for one season. Summer is the time when most people are out in the their garden, so summer bloomers, such as roses and jasmine, are the most popular. Spring bloomers include the glorious pink clematis Montana; in the fall, the pretty black-eyed Susan vine is in its glory. If you want coverage all year

Moonlight Parfait Mandevilla

long, consider evergreens, such as the Evergreen Clematis or honeysuckle. *Tip:* Plant several plants that bloom in different seasons along with evergreens so your structure has color all year round.

Day or night? Most vines are daytime bloomers; a few, such as the night blooming jasmine, prefer moonlight.

Sun or shade? Most vines adore sun. A few, such as climbing hydrangea and other woodland plants, are the oddballs that thrive in shade.

Color? Dazzling yellow, flaming crimson, royal purple, sky blue—the colors of vining plants are almost endless. Even flowerless ones like ivy have variegated species.

Show-off? The showiest flowers are clematis, wisteria, and roses. Clematis is the easiest of the three to grow; wisteria is suitable only for large sturdy structures; and everybody loves roses no matter how much effort they might need.

Growing zone? You may adore the flashy bougainvillea seen in travel photos of the Mediterranean, but if you live in the Rockies, you can't grow it. Know your growing zone requirements, and seek advice from local nurseries or gardening neighbors.

Time for maintenance? Just because arbor or trellis plants might be a distance from your back door doesn't mean they can survive without you. They all need watering, mulch, occasional fertilization, pruning, and praise for how fabulous they look.

How many times to plant? What do you do with a pressure treated arbor while you're waiting until you can paint it? Plant a fast-growing annual that you'll remove when the growing season is over. Then let it go bare, finish the arbor, and plant a permanent vine—easy!

Cecile Brunner Climbing Rose

Lavender Lady Passion Flower

Nelly Moser Clematis

Goldflame Honeysuckle

SUN-TOPPED PYRAMID TRELLIS

Adapted Design by Olivier Rollin

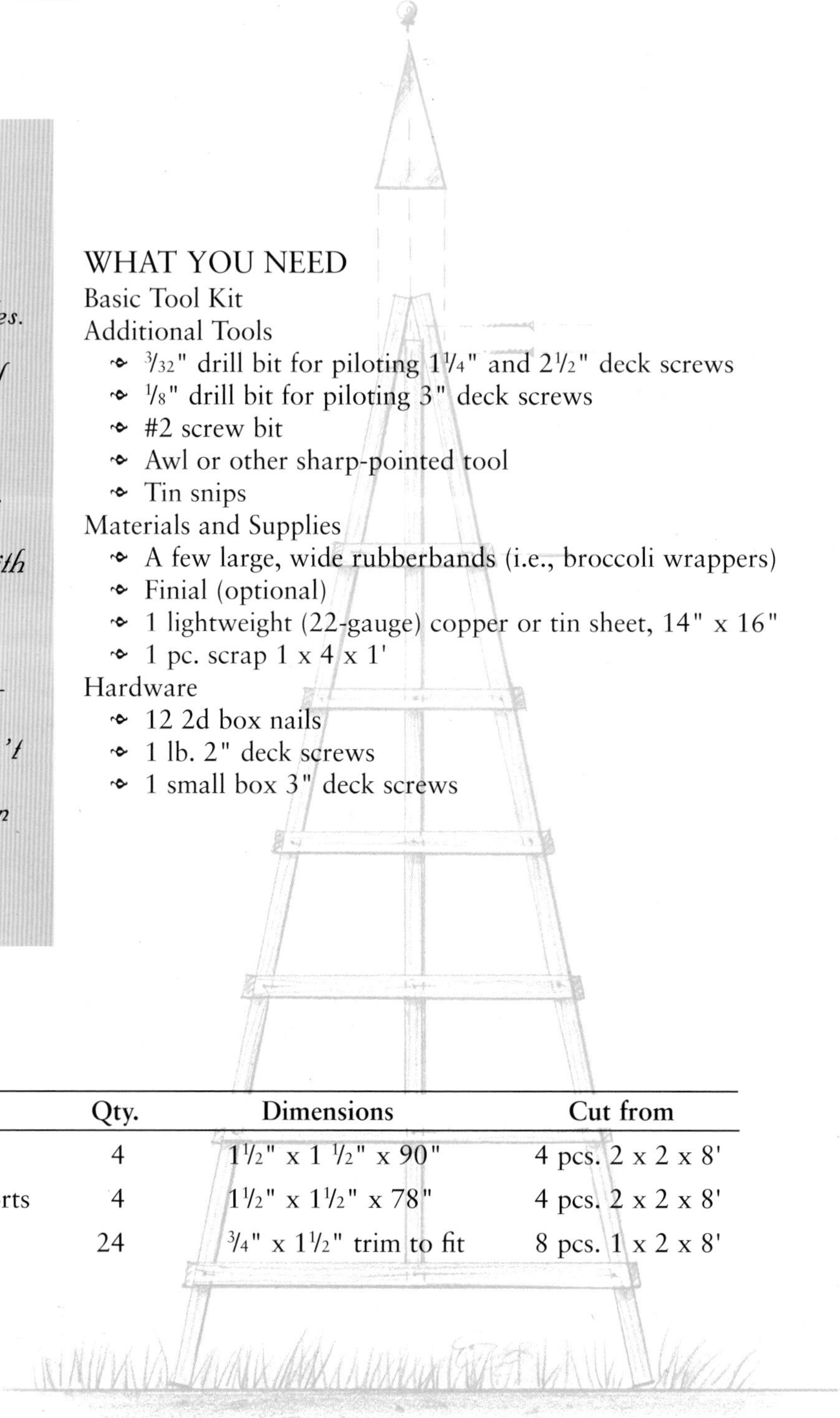

Like the ancient pyramids in Egypt, this portable trellis has four sides. Our version is easy to build because instead of making sophisticated compound cuts at the peak, we topped it with a decorative metal cap that gleams in the sun. The copper or tin for the cap doesn't need to be brand new; it can be recycled, even rusty.

WHAT YOU NEED

Basic Tool Kit

Additional Tools
- $3/32$" drill bit for piloting $1\frac{1}{4}$" and $2\frac{1}{2}$" deck screws
- $1/8$" drill bit for piloting 3" deck screws
- #2 screw bit
- Awl or other sharp-pointed tool
- Tin snips

Materials and Supplies
- A few large, wide rubberbands (i.e., broccoli wrappers)
- Finial (optional)
- 1 lightweight (22-gauge) copper or tin sheet, 14" x 16"
- 1 pc. scrap 1 x 4 x 1'

Hardware
- 12 2d box nails
- 1 lb. 2" deck screws
- 1 small box 3" deck screws

CUTTING LIST

Code	Description	Qty.	Dimensions	Cut from
A	Uprights	4	$1\frac{1}{2}$" x $1\frac{1}{2}$" x 90"	4 pcs. 2 x 2 x 8'
B	Middle Supports	4	$1\frac{1}{2}$" x $1\frac{1}{2}$" x 78"	4 pcs. 2 x 2 x 8'
C	Crosspieces	24	$3/4$" x $1\frac{1}{2}$" trim to fit	8 pcs. 1 x 2 x 8'

INSTRUCTIONS

Cutting and Marking the Pieces

1. Cut all the pieces (see fig. 1) to length, except for the crosspieces (C). You'll trim these pieces as you attach them to the trellis.

Gain a luxurious look with two vining plants on the same structure. Roses and honeysuckle make a beautiful duo.

2. Measuring from the bottom of one upright (A), make a mark every 10" for a total of six marks. Align the other three uprights next to the first, and duplicate the marks using the combination square.

Making the Sides

3. Choose a large flat working surface, such as your yard or driveway. Using figure 2 as a guide, position two of the uprights (A) with the marked sides facing up and their top ends even with each other. Make a temporary joint by securing the top ends together with rubber bands, as shown in figure 3. Using the tape measure, spread the bottom ends 38" apart.

4. Still referring to figure 2, take one of the crosspieces (C) and lay it on top of the joined uprights, with its upper edge on the lowest mark on the uprights. Let the crosspiece overhang an upright 1" or so at one end. Secure this end of the crosspiece by drilling a pilot hole and driving a 2" screw through the hole into the upright. Screw the opposite side of the crosspiece to the opposite upright in the same manner, checking that the uprights are still 38" apart. Use the handsaw to trim the short overhang of the crosspiece flush with the upright, using the side of the upright as a guide. Then trim the opposite, longer overhang in the same way, and set the offcut aside for use later. With the pencil and tape measure, mark the center of the crosspiece you just attached.

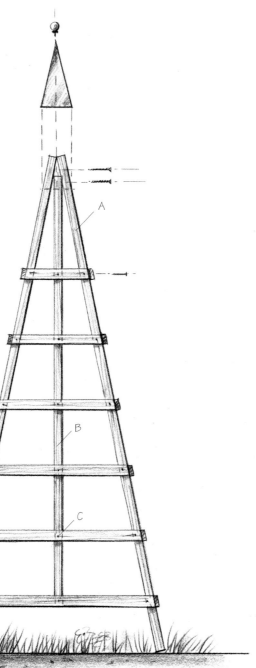

FIGURE 1: Sun-Topped Pyramid Trellis

5. Position one middle support (B) between the two uprights with its top end pushed as far as it will go against the uprights. Use the centermark on the bottom crosspiece to center the support. Secure the bottom end of the support to the crosspiece by drilling a pilot hole and driving a 2" screw through the support and into the crosspiece.

6. Once the middle support is in place, go back to the top of the assembly, drill pilot holes and drive 3" screws through the uprights and into the middle support. (See fig. 3.) Remove the rubber bands, then drill a pilot hole and drive one more 3" screw at the top of the assembly to attach the two uprights to each other.

7. Attach the remaining crosspieces. Retrieve the offcut from the first crosspiece you set aside in step 4. Align its top edge on the next two marks on the uprights, with its already sawn edge flush with the outside edge of one of the uprights. Secure it in place by drilling a pilot hole and driving a 2" screw. Then trim the opposite end with the handsaw, making it flush with the other upright.

8. Using the offcut and/or more crosspiece stock, nail and trim the remaining four crosspieces to complete one side.

9. Make the second side by repeating steps 3 through 8. You've now completed two sides of the pyramid.

Assembling the Pyramid

10. Call in your helper. Standing on the stepladder, hold the two completed sides upright so they meet at the top. Wrap rubber bands around the tops of the two

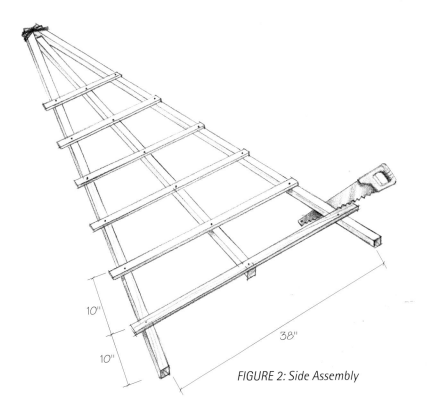

FIGURE 2: Side Assembly

10"
10"
38"

sides to temporarily hold them together. Spread the bottoms of the uprights 38" apart. When you're satisfied with their position, drill pilot holes and drive 3" screws through the tops of the uprights to connect the two sides. Take off the rubber bands.

11. Your helper's job is to hold the structure steady while you work. Repeat steps 4 and 5 to attach the remaining crosspieces (C) and two middle supports (B) to the open sides of the pyramid. Use the previously attached crosspieces as guides to align and trim the new pieces flush to the uprights.

12. At this point, go back to the top of the pyramid and drive a few more 3" screws to stiffen the joint. Remember that the joint needs to be strong, but it

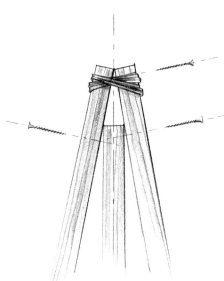

FIGURE 3: Joining the Top

doesn't have to look perfect because you are going to hide it with the beautiful cap.

Making the Decorative Cap

13. Referring to figure 4, lay out the cutting and bending pattern on your sheet of copper or tin. Using a string compass (see information on page 16), draw an arc with a 12" radius on the metal stock. Starting at one end of the arc, use a pencil compass to make five marks at 6" intervals along the line of the arc. Connect these marks with the centerpoint of the radius, and draw five straight lines, dividing the arc into four equal segments, as shown in figure 4. Finish laying out the sheet by drawing a ½" lip at the outer end of each segment, and draw another ½" lip along the edge of one of the outermost segments.

14. Use the tin snips to cut along your layout lines.

15. Working on a stout surface, such as a benchtop or piece of plywood on the floor, use a hammer to fold the four shorter ½" lips back upon each segment, creating folded seams that will stiffen the edge of the cap. On the corner of a piece of scrap wood, hammer and fold the longer ½" lip to about 90°.

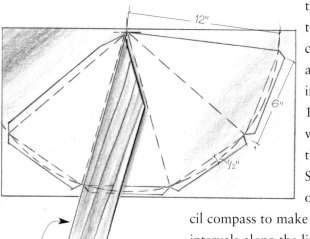

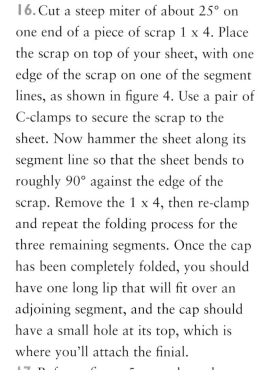

FIGURE 4: Laying Out the Cap

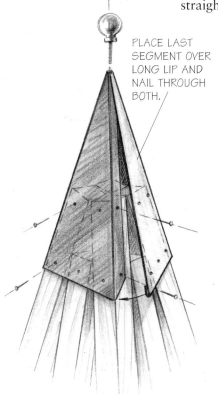

PLACE LAST SEGMENT OVER LONG LIP AND NAIL THROUGH BOTH.

FIGURE 5: Installing the Cap

16. Cut a steep miter of about 25° on one end of a piece of scrap 1 x 4. Place the scrap on top of your sheet, with one edge of the scrap on one of the segment lines, as shown in figure 4. Use a pair of C-clamps to secure the scrap to the sheet. Now hammer the sheet along its segment line so that the sheet bends to roughly 90° against the edge of the scrap. Remove the 1 x 4, then re-clamp and repeat the folding process for the three remaining segments. Once the cap has been completely folded, you should have one long lip that will fit over an adjoining segment, and the cap should have a small hole at its top, which is where you'll attach the finial.

17. Refer to figure 5 to see how the cap fits over the top of the pyramid. Once you've positioned the cap, secure it to the uprights and the middle supports with the 2d nails. Use an awl or a sharp pointed tool and a hammer to perforate the metal before you drive the nails. If you use copper for the cap, consider using copper nails.

18. With the cap in place, insert a finial or other decorative item into the hole at the top of the cap. (A new or vintage drawer pull would be great.) Add a drop of silicone adhesive in the hole, then insert the stud or bolt of the finial into the hole and let the adhesive cure.

19. Once the finial is secured, with your helper carry the trellis to the spot of your choice. If you don't like it there next season—move it again!

TRADITIONAL FAN TRELLIS

Adapted Design by Olivier Rollin

Conjure up nostalgic images of cottage gardens and croquet games on the lawn with this traditional fan trellis. We simplified the classic design by reducing the number of crosspieces and overlapping their ends instead of mitering them.

WHAT YOU NEED

Basic Tool Box

Additional Tools

- ↪ ¹⁄₃₂" drill bit for piloting 6d and 8d nails

Materials and Supplies

- ↪ 9 ready-made lattice strips, ¼" x 1½" x 8' long for the ribs and crosspieces
- ↪ 2 support blocks of scrap 2 x 4, approximately 12" long

Hardware

- ↪ ½ lb. 6d nails
- ↪ 1 8d nail
- ↪ A few screws or nails to attach the trellis to the wall

INSTRUCTIONS

Assembling the Ribs

1. Measure seven of the lattice pieces for the ribs, or vertical pieces, of the fan. With the handsaw, cut the ribs 72" long.

2. Refer to figure 1 to measure and mark square lines across the front of one of the ribs.

3. Stack all seven ribs, placing the marked one on top and aligning all the pieces with each other. Drill a pilot hole through the stack at the middle of the first mark, 8" from the end, as shown in figure 2. This hole will act as a pivot for an 8d nail.

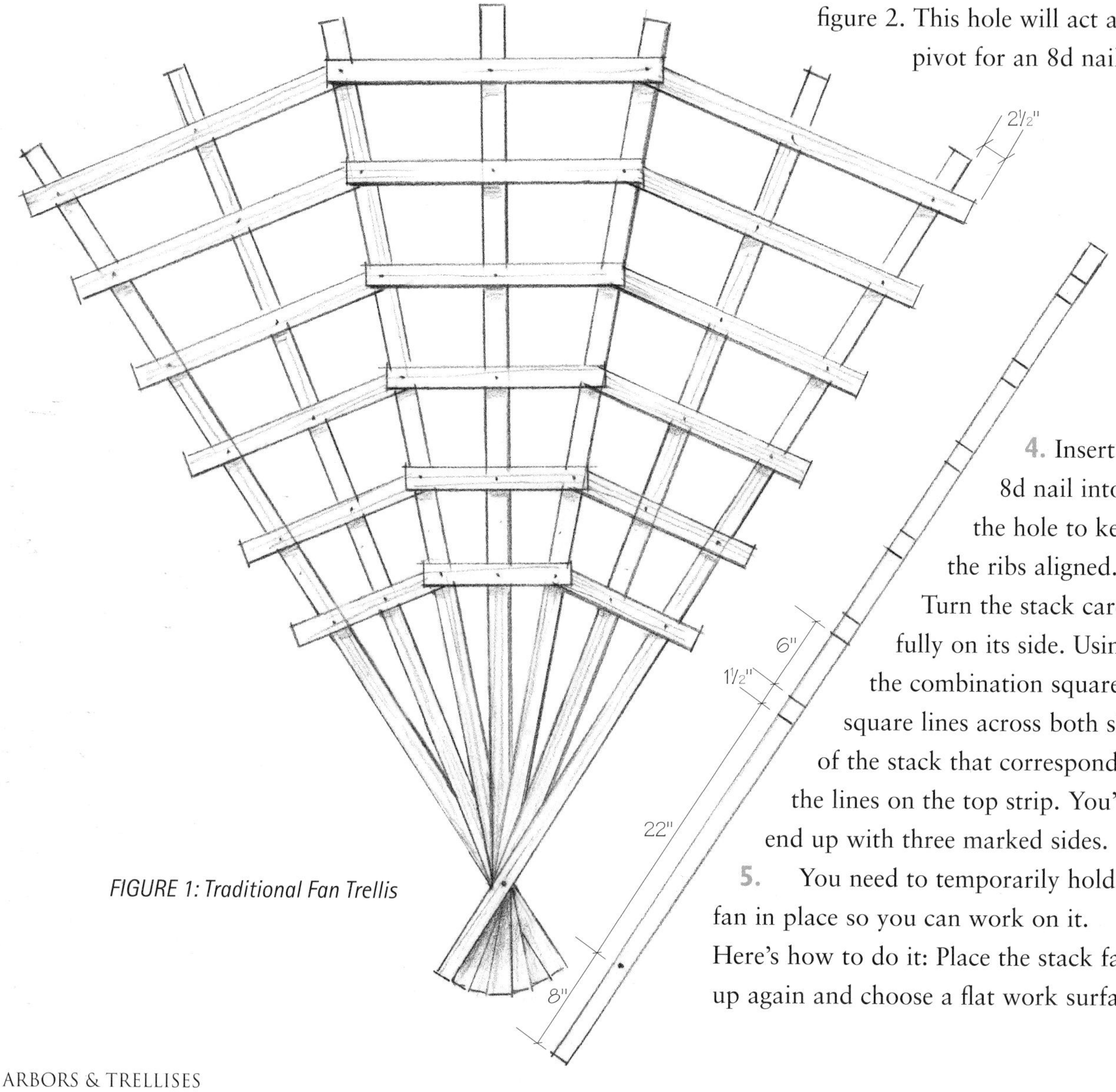

FIGURE 1: Traditional Fan Trellis

4. Insert an 8d nail into the hole to keep the ribs aligned. Turn the stack carefully on its side. Using the combination square, square lines across both sides of the stack that correspond to the lines on the top strip. You'll end up with three marked sides.

5. You need to temporarily hold the fan in place so you can work on it. Here's how to do it: Place the stack face up again and choose a flat work surface,

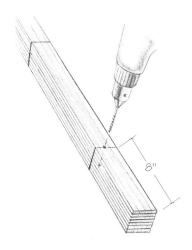

FIGURE 2: Drilling the Pivot Hole

such as a piece of plywood or an outdoor picnic table into which you can drive nails without regret. Drive the 8d nail into the work surface to secure one end of the stack. Using the nail as a pivot point, spread the stack into a fan shape, spacing the tops of the ribs 12" apart. (See fig.1.) Hold each rib in position by driving a 6d nail through its top end and partway into the work surface.

Attaching the Crosspieces

6. The next step is to cut and attach the crosspieces. Work one row at a time and use the mark on the ribs to guide you. Measure and cut each crosspiece so its end extends slightly past each rib. Where a crosspiece meets an outer rib, let its end extend about 2½" past the rib, as shown in figure 1. When two crosspieces meet at a rib location, cut the second crosspiece so it overlaps the first, as shown in figure 3. Because the ribs are stacked together at the bottom of the fan, some of the crosspieces will be raised above the surface and you'll have

to push them down to facilitate the nailing. Don't worry, the structure is flexible.

7. Drill pilot holes and drive 6d nails through all the joints, tapping the nails just enough so they go through the joints but not deep into the work surface. When all the joints are nailed, carefully lift the fan off the work surface. Then slip scrap blocks under the joints for support, and finish driving the nails all the way through the pieces, as shown in figure 4.

8. Carefully flip the fan over (watch those sharp nail ends!) and bend the protruding nails with the hammer, clinching the nails and securing the joints.

Installing the Trellis

9. Attach the trellis to its final location on the wall with the appropriate screws or nails. The only problem with fan trellises is they're so attractive it seems you can never have just one. Make several and decorate a fence with a whole fan dance!

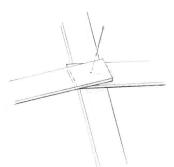

FIGURE 3: Overlapping the Joints

FIGURE 4: Nailing with Support Blocks

Impatient for real flowers to start climbing up the wall? Paint them on!

PORCH PRIVACY TRELLIS

Adapted Design by Olivier Rollin

Create privacy and shade, yet still enjoy a garden view and the pleasure of being outside. No need for a workshop— you can make this handsome trellis right there on your porch.

WHAT YOU NEED

Basic Tool Box
Additional Tools
- $3/32$" drill bit for piloting $1/2$" and $3/4$" screws
- Jigsaw
- Circular saw (optional)

Materials and Supplies
- Masking tape
- Water-resistant wood glue
- 8 metal corner braces (The exact size of the braces will be determined by the clearance you leave between the trellis frame and the wall.)
- Contractor paper (heavy-duty brown paper in a 35" wide roll, available at home improvement stores)

Hardware
- 1 lb. $1/2$" deck screws
- 1 lb. $3/4$" deck screws
- 1 lb. $1 1/4$ deck screws

CUTTING LIST

Code	Description	Qty.	Dimensions	Cut from
A	Arch	1	Inside Radius: $10 1/4$" Outside Radius: $11 3/4$"	1 sheet of $3/4$ x 2 x 4' plywood
B	Gussets	10	$3/4$" x $1 1/2$" x 4"	Plywood left over from the arch
C	Frame			8 pcs. 1 x 2 x 8' for all the frame
C-1	Top Crosspiece	1	$3/4$" x $1 1/2$ x 67"	parts, C-1 through C-5.
C-2	Side Uprights	2	$3/4$" x $1 1/2$ x 90"	
C-3	Middle Uprights	2	$3/4$" x $1 1/2$" x $59 1/2$"	
C-4	Bottom Crosspieces	2	$3/4$" x $1 1/2$ x 20"	
C-5	Centerpiece	1	$3/4$" x $1 1/2$ x $21 1/2$"	
D	Lattice Strips	55	$1/4$" x $1 1/2$" trim to fit	20 pcs. $1/4$" x $1 1/2$" x 8'**

**Usually available in 16' lengths. But they can be cut in half in the store for easy transportation home.

Note: The trellis is protected by a porch ceiling, so you don't need to use pressure treated (PT) wood. If you choose to forgo PT wood, you can paint the trellis without having to wait for the wood to season. In fact, you might want to paint the pieces before you assemble them, then plan on touching up any unpainted areas after assembly.

The trellis is designed to fit the end of a porch, between the wall of the house and the porch's corner post or wall. The cutting list calls for a trellis that is 66" wide by 90" high; adapt the measurements to fit your particular porch. Build the frame so there's plenty of clearance between your walls, floor, ceiling, and columns so you can lift it easily and fit it into place. A clearance of ½" for each side of the frame is sufficient. For example, between a floor and a ceiling you should allow 1" extra space for the frame.

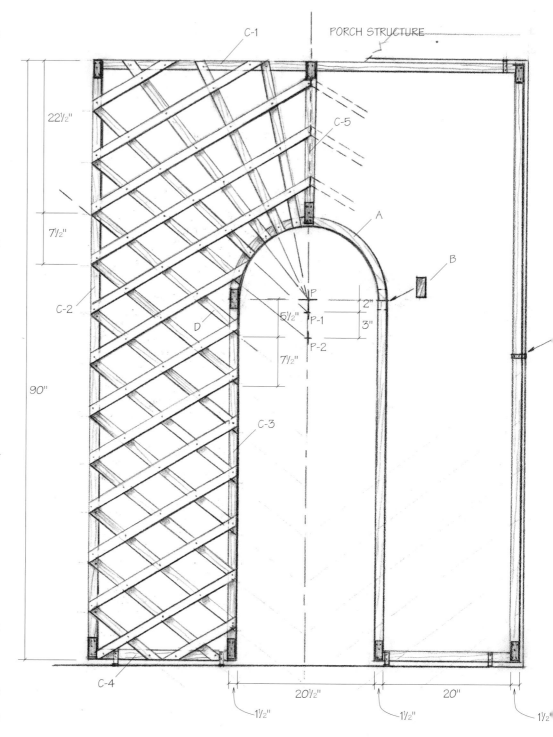

FIGURE 1: *Porch Privacy Trellis*

INSTRUCTIONS

Preparing the Work Area

1. To help with construction and protect your porch floor, lay down two 120" lengths of contractor paper side by side on the floor. Tape across the joints where they meet using masking tape, and secure the perimeter of the assembled sheet to the floor with more tape. The sheet's centerline will be used as a guide during construction.

Making the Arch

2. Refer to the instructions on page 16 on how to use a trammel. Draw the inner and outer radii of the arch (A) on the plywood as listed in the cutting list. With the jigsaw, cut out the arch piece and set it aside.

Cutting the Gussets and the Frame Pieces

3. Using the leftover plywood from the arch, measure and cut out the 10 gussets (B) with the handsaw or the circular saw.

4. Cut all the frame pieces (C-1 through C-5) to length. Measure and plan your cuts in order to make the longer cuts from full-length stock so that you can make the shorter cuts from the lumber that remains.

Building the Frame

5. Lay out all the pieces of the frame in rough order on the paper sheet, as shown in figure 2, including the arch (A), the gussets (B), and the frame pieces (C). All the joints of the frame are butt joints reinforced with the gussets, as shown in figure 3.

6. With the frame parts laid out, construct one joint at a time. It's best if you start by joining the outer perimeter of the frame, then work toward the center, finishing with the arch (A) and the centerpiece (C-5). Brush glue on all the adjoining surfaces, then attach the gusset to one leg of the joint by drilling pilot holes and driving 1¼" screws through the gusset and into the frame piece. Position the adjoining leg under the gusset and secure the joint with a C-clamp. Check the joint with the framing square. Drill pilot holes and drive 1¼" screws to secure the joint. Wipe off any excess glue and remove the clamp. Complete all the other joints in the same manner. As your work progresses, measure from the centerline on the paper to gauge that your work is straight and square. Let the glue dry.

Attaching the Bottom Layer of Lattice Strips

7. As shown in figure 1, lay out and attach one half of the lattice strips (D) at a time, beginning with the bottom layer of lattice, or the layer closest to the frame. Start by marking the outside edge of one side upright (C-2) 22½" from the top of the frame. On the inside edge of the corresponding middle upright (C-3), make a mark 5½" from the bottom end of the arch, as shown in figure 1. From these two marks, measure and mark the

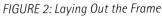

FIGURE 2: Laying Out the Frame

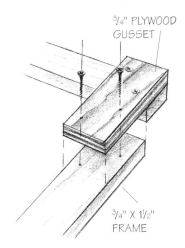

¾" PLYWOOD GUSSET

¾" X 1½" FRAME

FIGURE 3: Frame Joint Detail

uprights at intervals of 7½" to the bottom of the frame.

8. Lay down the first angled lattice strip (D) with its bottom edge on the uppermost marks you made in the previous step, as shown in figure 1. At this point, cut the strip to rough length, letting both ends extend slightly past the uprights. (You'll trim all the strips flush with the frame later.) Where each end of the lattice strip overlaps an upright, drill a pilot hole and drive a single ¾" screw through the strip and into the upright. With the first strip secured, cut the second strip to rough length and position it below the first, aligning it with the second set of marks you made on the uprights. Attach the strip by drilling pilot holes and driving ¾" screws as before. Continue cutting the strips to rough length and attaching them with screws until you reach the bottom of the frame.

9. Add the five lattice strips (D) that fan out at the top of the frame, as shown in figure 1. Position the strips so they fan out in an even pattern. You can eyeball their positions if you wish. Or for a more precise layout, use the center of the arch (shown as P in figure 1) to help position the three uppermost strips. Mark the arch's center on the paper sheet, then pull a length of string taut from the center and over the frame, making equidistant marks on the top crosspiece (C-1). Secure the three lattice pieces on your marks. To lay out and secure the two remaining strips, use points P-1 and P-2 as centerpoints for your string, as shown in figure 1.

10. On the centerpiece (C-5), cut and attach a lattice strip (D) between the top and bottom gussets (B) to compensate for the thickness of the first layer. Drill pilot holes, spread glue on the adjoining surfaces, and attach the strip with ¾" screws. This built-up layer will accommodate the second, top layer of lattice strips. You've now completed the bottom layer of lattice strips for one side of the trellis.

11. Repeat steps 7 through 10 to attach the bottom layer of lattice strips to the opposite side. Once all the bottom layers of strips are secured, use a handsaw or the circular saw to trim the rough-cut strips flush with the frame.

Attaching the Top Layer of Lattice Strips

12. To position the top lattice strips (D), use the points where the bottom strips intersect with the frame. Reverse the angle on the top strips so that they crisscross with the bottom layer, as shown on figure 1. All the strips on the top layer are simply laid parallel with each other and spaced equally apart. As before, attach the strips in rough length, then go back and trim the strips flush to the frame once they're secured. Use ¾" screws to secure the strips where they attach to the frame; use ½" screws where the lattice strips intersect with the strips from the bottom layer. Attach this layer to the frame with glue and 1¼" screws; at the points where the lattice strips cross the bottom layer, secure with ½" screws. To back up the joints, place a piece of scrap 1 x 2 under each joint when you're driving the screw.

13. Six lattice strips on the top layer are attached to the centerpiece (C-5). Use the handsaw to miter one end of each strip so they meet at a miter joint in the center of the trellis. Test the fit of the joints before attaching the strips to the frame.

Installing the Trellis

14. Lay out the trellis where it will be attached. Using the carpenter's level, draw a vertical plumb line down the wall where the trellis will go. Mark a similar plumb line on the opposite wall or column. At the center of each line, attach a metal corner brace. On the floor, draw a connecting line between the bottoms of the vertical lines. Use the tops of the vertical lines to draw a connecting line on the ceiling. Attach a corner brace in the center of the top and bottom lines. (The material of your walls and posts determine the types of screws or anchors you use to secure the braces.) You now have four braces secured to the porch.

15. With your helper, stand up the screen against the corner braces. The floor of your porch is probably slanted to handle rain runoff. Use small blocks of scrap wood of different thicknesses to shim the bottom of the trellis off the floor and keep it parallel to the wall.

16. With your helper holding the screen firmly in place, drill pilot holes and drive 3/4" screws through each corner brace and into the perimeter of the trellis frame to secure it firmly in place. Remove the shim blocks. Pull up a cushioned chair and let the breeze through the lattice cool you for the entire summer.

Variation

SMALL PORCH SCREEN

For a small porch, assemble this simple screen. Measure and cut all the pieces. Screw or nail together an outer frame consisting of three 2 x 4s (attach one to the house) and a 4 x 4 as a sturdy outside post. Sandwich a readymade sheet of 1/4" lattice between an inner frame of eight pieces of 1x stock, nailing the stock to the outer frame on both sides of the lattice. Instant privacy!

ART DECO LATTICE TRELLIS

Design by Mark Strom

Lattice and more lattice! Give your garden a stunning piece of trellis sculpture with this geometric design based on the distinctive Art Deco style.

WHAT YOU NEED

Basic Tool Kit

Additional Tools
- ⌁ ³/₆₄" drill bit for piloting 4d nails
- ⌁ ¹/₁₆" drill bit for piloting 6d nails
- ⌁ ¹/₈" drill bit for piloting 3" screws
- ⌁ Jigsaw or coping saw with a fine blade

Materials and Supplies
- ⌁ 1 piece of cardboard, 24" x 24"

Hardware
- ⌁ 5 lbs. 4d finish nails
- ⌁ 32 6d finish nails
- ⌁ 12 3" decking screws

CUTTING LIST

Code	Description	Qty.	Dimensions	Cut from
A	Frame Pieces	2	3½" x 3½" x 102"	2 pcs. 4 x 4 x 10'
B	Crosspieces	8	1½" x 1½" x 48"	2 pcs. 2 x 2 x 6'
C	Spacers	2	³/₄" X 1½" X 48"	21 pcs. 1 x 2 x 8'
D	Uprights	6	³/₄" x 1½" x 96"	for all the lattice pieces,
E	Curved Lattice Pieces	4	³/₄" x 1½" x 48"	C through K
F	Short Spacers	4	³/₄" x 1½" x 3'	
G	28" Lattice	5	³/₄" x 1½" x 28"	
H	18" Lattice	16	³/₄" x 1½" x 18"	
I	7" Lattice	16	³/₄" x 1½" x 7"	
J	10³/₄" Lattice	2	³/₄" x 1½" x 10³/₄"	
K	8" Lattice	2	³/₄" x 1½" x 8"	
L	Stakes	2	1½ x 1½ x 72"	2 pcs. 2 x 2 x 8'

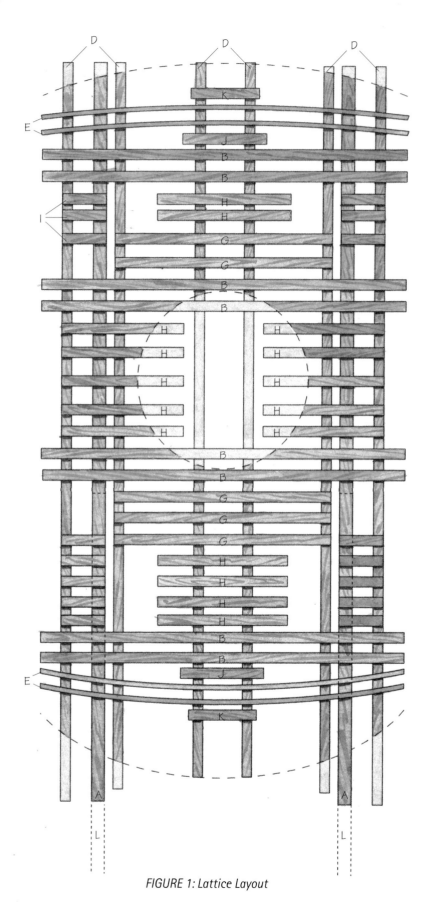

FIGURE 1: Lattice Layout

INSTRUCTIONS

Cutting the Pieces

1. Start by cutting all the pieces from the 1 x 2, 2 x 2, and 4 x 4 stock, cutting the longest pieces from the straightest stock.

2. On each frame piece (A), measure up from the bottom and mark two lines, one at 17¼" and one at 44¼". Measuring down from the top, mark each frame piece at 9" and at 26¼". On the crosspieces (B), measure and mark 5" in from each end.

Constructing the Frame Pieces and Crosspieces

3. Position the frame pieces (A) parallel to each other. Place four crosspieces (B) across them, two with their lower edges at the 17¼" and 4½" marks, and two with their upper edges at the 9" and 26¼" marks. Align the 5" marks on each crosspiece with the outer edge of each frame piece. Then fasten the crosspieces in place with three 3d finish nails at each joint. (All perpendicular pieces in this project are fastened in the same manner.)

4. Set one spacer (C), which won't be a part of the finished trellis, below the crosspiece (B) at the 9" mark, edge to edge, with its wide face down. Place another spacer below the crosspiece at the 26¼" mark. Then place a crosspiece edge to edge below each spacer, leaving a 5" overlap at each end. Fasten the two crosspieces to the frame pieces (A) and remove the spacers.

5. Set one spacer (C) above the crosspiece (B) at the 17¼" mark and another above the crosspiece at the 44¼" mark. Then place a crosspiece above each spacer, fasten the crosspieces as before, and remove the spacers.

6. Turn the assembly over so the frame pieces (A) face up.

Attaching the Uprights

7. Measure and mark each attached crosspiece (B) 2" out from the outer edge of each frame piece (A).

8. Position a vertical upright (D) on the assembly, with its inner edge at one set of the 2" marks on the crosspieces (B). Position a second upright on the other side of the assembly, aligning it with the 2" marks on the crosspieces on that side. Adjust both uprights so their ends are aligned with the ends of the frame pieces (A). Then nail both uprights in place.

9. Place a spacer (C), wide face down, against the inner edge of each frame piece (A). Then place another upright (D) with its outer edge against each spacer's inner edge. Adjust the uprights so their top ends are 1" taller than the ends of the frame pieces. (Their top ends will be 10" above the topmost crosspiece [B].) Nail both uprights in place, and remove the spacers.

10. Measuring in from the inner edge of each upright (D) that you attached in step 9, mark each crosspiece (B) at 10".

11. Position the two remaining uprights (D) with their outer edges at the 10" marks on the crosspieces (B), which will leave about 4" between these center uprights. Position them so that their top ends are 12" above the topmost crosspiece. Nail these uprights in place.

Securing the Curved Lattice Pieces

12. Turn the assembly over again, so the crosspieces (B) are facing up.

13. Place the short spacers (F) on edge along the two middle uprights (D), with one end of each against the top crosspiece (B). Lay a curved lattice (E) on edge across the uprights (D), and push it against the short spacers. At this point the curved lattice is still straight, and its ends should line up with the ends of the crosspieces.

14. Place a scrap of 1 x 2 under the uprights (D) to support them while drilling and nailing. Bore a pilot hole through the edge of the curved lattice (E) centered over each of the two middle uprights. Drive a 6d finish nail through each of these holes into the middle uprights. Use a nail set to sink the nails deeper.

15. Place a spacer (C) across each outside upright (D) to form a 1½" space above the ends of the uppermost crosspiece (B). Clamp one end of the curved lattice (E) where it is, to the outside upright. Bend the other end of the curved lattice until it touches the spacer. Clamp the end of the curved lattice to the spacer and to the end of the crosspiece.

16. Unclamp, bend, and clamp the first end of the curved lattice (E) to the other spacer (C) and to the end of the crosspiece (B).

The Evergreen Clematis is a perfect quick grower for lattice trellises. It has fragrant star-like blooms that flower in the spring.

17. Bore two pilot holes at opposing angles through the edge of the curved lattice (E) and barely into each of the frame pieces (A) and uprights (D), including the two middle uprights. Drive 6d finish nails into the holes and set them well. Remove the clamps and spacers.

18. Use a spacer (C) to position another curved lattice (E) 1½" above the first one and clamp it in place. Use two 6d finish nails driven through pilot holes at opposing angles to fasten the curved lattice to each frame piece (A) and upright (D).

19. Repeat steps 13 through 18 to attach the other two curved lattices (E) below the bottom crosspiece (B).

Attaching the Lattice

20. Using a spacer (C), and referring to figure 1, attach the five 28" lattices (G) to the center and inner uprights (D). Be sure the ends of these lattices are even, and that each lattice is centered across the uprights.

21. Take a good look at figure 1 on page 50. There are four 18" lattices (H) centered across the middle uprights (D) at the bottom of the trellis. Using a spacer (C) and working downward, nail the upper three lattices in place. Position the fourth (and lowest) lattice by centering it in the space between the third lattice and the crosspiece (B) beneath it.

22. To attach the two lattices (H) at the top of the trellis, first use a spacer (C) to position one above the uppermost 28" lattice (G). After nailing it in place, turn the spacer on edge and place one face

against the lattice you just fastened. Then position the second 28" lattice above the spacer, and nail it in place.

23. As you can see in figure 1, in the center of the trellis there are ten 18" lattices (H) attached to the outermost and middle uprights (D) and to the frame pieces (A). Using a spacer (C) and working downward, first fasten the top two lattices on each side and then the bottom two on each side, aligning one end of each with the outside edge of an outer upright. Center each of the two remaining lattices in the space that remains and nail them in place.

24. To attach all the 7" lattices (I) to the outer uprights (D) and frame pieces (A), as shown in figure 1, just align each one with the lattice to its left or right.

25. At the top and bottom of the trellis, below the curved lattices (E) at the top, and above the curved lattices at the bottom, center a 10¾" lattice (J) and nail it in place.

26. Using a short spacer (F) placed on its edge, center and fasten an 8" lattice (K) across the innermost uprights (D), above the curved lattices (E) at the top of the trellis. Repeat to attach another 8" lattice below the curved lattices at the bottom. (Both these lattices will overlap the innermost uprights.)

Laying Out and Cutting the Curves

27. Use the trammel to draw a 22"-diameter circle on the piece of cardboard, and cut out the circle with a utility knife. Using figure 1 as a guide, place the cardboard circle in the middle of the trellis and trace around it. Then cut out the circle with a jigsaw or a coping saw.

28. At the top of the trellis, use a jigsaw or a coping saw to trim off the ends of the four outermost uprights (D) and the frame pieces (A) to form a gentle arc. (The dashed lines on figure 1 show where to cut.) Don't trim the two uprights in the center of the trellis.

29. At the bottom of the trellis, use the jigsaw to trim the ends of all six uprights (D) as shown in figure 1, but don't trim the frame pieces (A).

Installing the Trellis

30. Place a stake (L) face-to-face against the back face of each frame piece (A), with 30" of the stake extending beyond the bottom end of the frame piece. Drill pilot holes and screw through each stake into the adjoining frame piece, using six evenly spaced 3" screws.

31. To install the trellis, dig two 30"-deep holes, spaced to accommodate the stakes (L). Place the bottom ends of the stakes in the holes; tightly pack the holes with dirt. Relax in a comfy spot where you can enjoy the late afternoon sun casting fascinating shadows through the lattice to the wall beyond.

Note: Even pressure treated lumber will eventually succumb to rot, particularly if it's in direct contact with moist earth. When the buried portions of the stakes begin to rot, simply dig up the trellis, unscrew the old stakes, and replace them with new ones.

HISTORICAL HIGHLIGHTS
of Arbors and Trellises

ARBOR COMES FROM the Latin word for tree, signifying this structure's basic purpose, to give shade as a tree does.

TRELLIS EVOLVED FROM a Latin phrase referring to fabric woven of triple threads.

OVER 2000 YEARS AGO, Chinese farmers began to grow grapes in a valley on the western face of the Flaming Mountains near Turpan, an ancient trading center. Today thousands of arbors continue to produce the seedless white grapes that become prized raisins.

IN THE THIRD CENTURY B.C. the Greek Sicilian ruler, King Hiero II had a garden full of ivy and grape arbors made on the deck of an enormous ship. Helping him landscape was his relative, the mathematician Archimedes of "Eureka! I found it!" fame.

GARDENS IN MEDIEVAL EUROPE were enclosed in trellis-covered protective walls. Reflecting belief that life led directly to God, the walkways were always straight or intersected in the shape of a cross.

ON THE OTHER HAND, traditional Islamic fountain-centered gardens had winding paths, often leading to an arbor which was tiled in bright colors. This type of arbor appeared in later Spanish gardens, called a glorietta.

AT HIS ROCOCO PALACE in Rheinberg, the young Fredrick the Great of Bavaria built a vineyard labyrinth that centered on a statue of Bacchus. It had to be covered in glass during the winter to protect its orange trees and pomegranates.

FOR PERFORMANCES OF THE STOMP DANCE, a traditional Cherokee religious dance, seven arbors are set up around the fire and dance area. Each arbor, made of large poles and covered with brush, represents one of the seven clans.

GABLE ARBOR
Adapted Design by Olivier Rollin

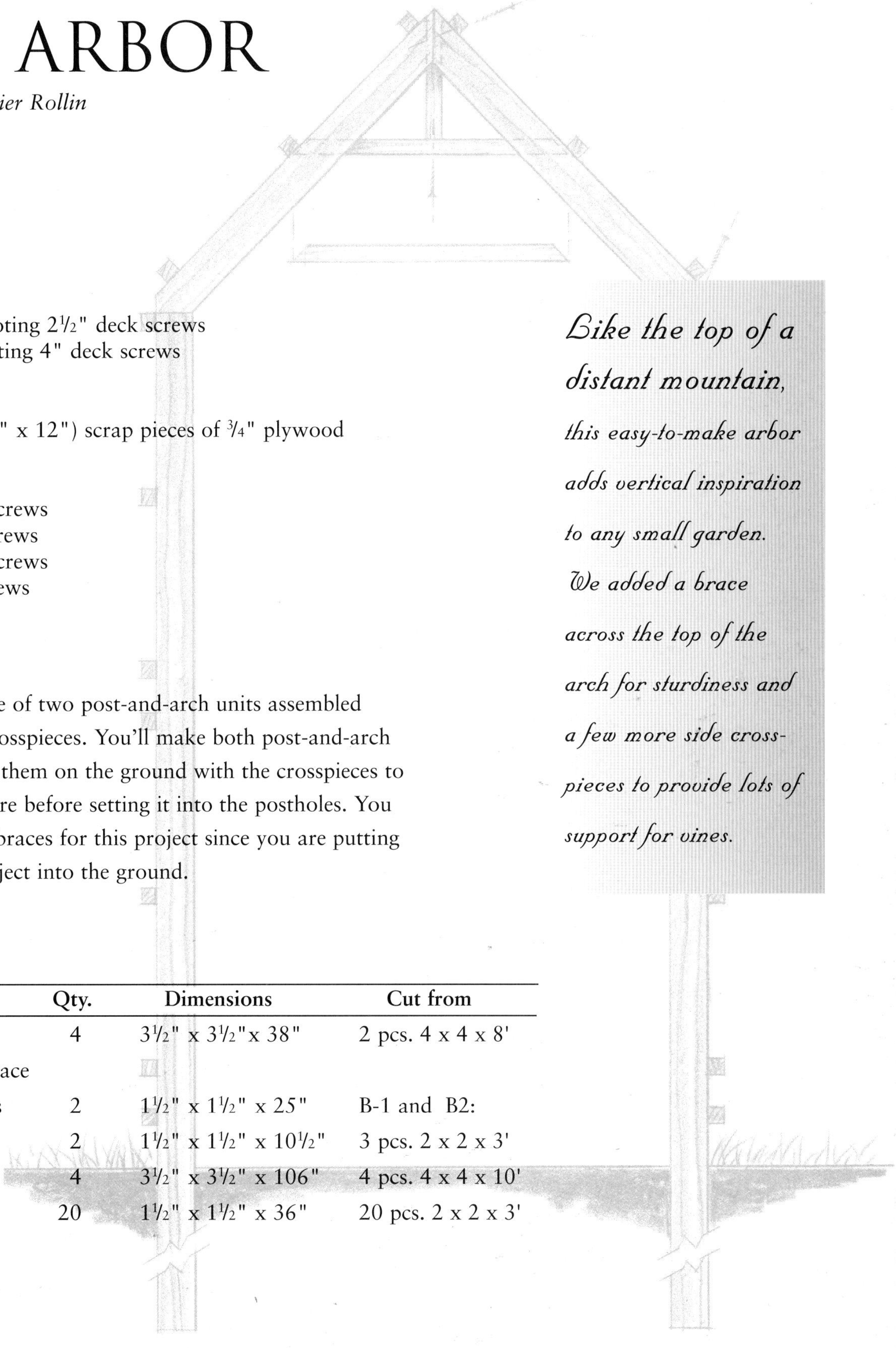

WHAT YOU NEED
Basic Tool Kit
Digging Kit
Additional Tools
- $^3/_{32}$" drill bit for piloting 2½" deck screws
- $^1/_8$" drill bit for piloting 4" deck screws
- Circular saw

Materials and Supplies
- 2 small (roughly 12" x 12") scrap pieces of ¾" plywood
- Crossbraces

Hardware
- 1 lb. of 2½" deck screws
- 1 lb. of 3" decks screws
- 1 lb. of 3½" deck screws
- 1 lb. of 4" deck screws

Note: This arbor is made of two post-and-arch units assembled together with the side crosspieces. You'll make both post-and-arch units first, and assemble them on the ground with the crosspieces to make a complete structure before setting it into the postholes. You don't need ground post braces for this project since you are putting the entire assembled project into the ground.

Like the top of a distant mountain, this easy-to-make arbor adds vertical inspiration to any small garden. We added a brace across the top of the arch for sturdiness and a few more side cross-pieces to provide lots of support for vines.

CUTTING LIST

Code	Description	Qty.	Dimensions	Cut from
A	Arch Pieces	4	3½" x 3½" x 38"	2 pcs. 4 x 4 x 8'
B	Decorative Brace			
B-1	Bottom Pieces	2	1½" x 1½" x 25"	B-1 and B2:
B-2	Centerpieces	2	1½" x 1½" x 10½"	3 pcs. 2 x 2 x 3'
C	Posts	4	3½" x 3½" x 106"	4 pcs. 4 x 4 x 10'
D	Crosspieces	20	1½" x 1½" x 36"	20 pcs. 2 x 2 x 3'

INSTRUCTIONS
Cutting the Pieces

1. Cut all the pieces to size according to the cutting list.

2. The four arch pieces (A) and the two bottom pieces (B-1) have 45° miter cuts at both ends. Take care when making these cuts because the success of the arbor depends on a tight fit of these joints. The lengths in the cutting list refer to the measurements from long point to long point of the miters. You'll trim one mitered end of each arch later.

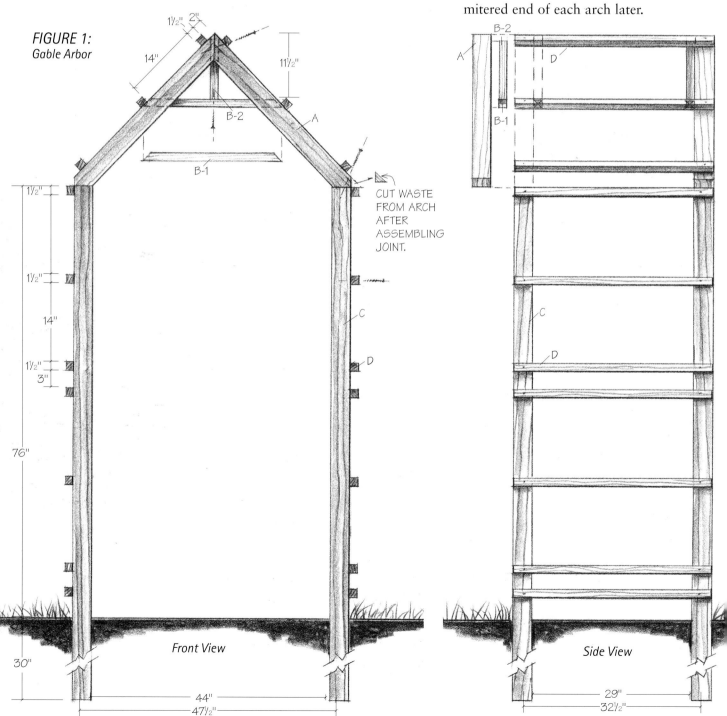

FIGURE 1:
Gable Arbor

CUT WASTE FROM ARCH AFTER ASSEMBLING JOINT.

Front View

Side View

Assembling the Arches

3. On a flat surface, position a pair of arch pieces (A). Align the miters at the top of the arch. Temporarily hold the joint together by laying a piece of scrap plywood across the arch pieces and clamping it in place with 6" C-clamps. Drill pilot holes 2½" from the top of the miter and drive the two 4" screws to secure the joint, as shown in figure 1.

4. Refer to figure 1 and make a mark on both arch pieces 11½" from the top of the miter to locate the bottom piece (B-1). Position the top edge of the bottom piece on your marks, as shown in figure 1. Drill pilot holes through the miters at both ends of the piece, making sure that the bottom of the arch is spread apart 44" then secure the piece to the arch assembly with 2½" screws.

5. As shown on figure 1, position the centerpiece (B-2) between the bottom piece and the top of the arch, centering it with the miter joint of the arch. Hold the centerpiece to the arch with C-clamps. Drill pilot holes through the bottom piece and through the upper end of the centerpiece. Drive a single 2½" screw through the underside of the bottom piece and into the centerpiece, then drive two 2½" screws through the upper end of the centerpiece and into the arch. Angle these screws slightly so they go into the arch assembly on either side of its miter joint.

6. Repeat steps 3 through 5 to construct the other arch.

Attaching the Arch to the Posts

7. On the ground, place 2 x 4 scraps and position one arch assembly and two posts (C) on top of the scraps. Align the miter cuts on the arch with the ends of the posts, such that the long points of the miters overhang each post. Check that the inside face of each post is flush with the inside face of the arch, and that the posts are parallel to each other. (See fig. 2.) Use scrap pieces of plywood and C-clamps to temporarily hold the miter joints together. Before moving to the next step, use a pencil and a combination square to draw the cut lines that you'll follow to trim the arch overhang even with the posts later. (See fig. 2.)

8. Drill two pilot holes for two 4" screws at each joint. (See fig. 1.) Position the holes close to, but not on the cutting lines you just drew in step 7. Drive the screws through the pilot holes and into the posts to secure the joints.

9. Attach crossbraces to the posts to temporarily brace them. Refer to the bracing information on page 28.

10. With the handsaw, cut the overhanging arch ends flush with the outside faces of the posts, as shown in figures 1 and 2.

11. Repeat steps 7 through 10 for the other post-and-arch assembly.

Attaching the Crosspieces

12. Refer to figure 1 for the locations of the crosspieces (D). To mark these locations on the sides of the post-and-arch-assemblies, stack the assemblies on top of each other and mark both at the same time.

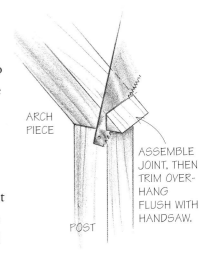

ARCH PIECE

ASSEMBLE JOINT, THEN TRIM OVERHANG FLUSH WITH HANDSAW.

POST

FIGURE 2: Arch-to-Post Joint

The spectacular mauve and blue Veilchenblau rose, "Blue Rambler," makes an astonishing display in early summer.

Time is what gives an arbor its true beauty. Shortly after construction, an arbor seems quite plain.

Six months later the arbor is in its glory, covered with roses and surrounded by other flowers.

13. Call in your helpers. Place scrap 2 x 4s on the ground, then place the post-and-arch assemblies on their sides on top of the scraps, facing each other. Position each crosspiece on the appropriate mark on the exposed side of the post-and-arch assembly, drill pilot holes 2" from its ends, and secure each crosspiece with 2½" screws. As you secure them in place, make sure the ends of the crosspieces are flush with the outside faces of the posts and the arches.

Installing the Arbor

14. See Preparing the Site (page 23) and Digging Postholes on page 26 in the basics section, and refer to project figure 1 (page 56) for dimensions. Dig the four postholes.

15. Call in your helper. Stand the arbor upright and carefully place it in the postholes. Use the carpenter's level to check that the structure is plumb. If necessary, adjust the height of the posts by adding more gravel at the bottom of the holes. Backfill around the posts, then remove the temporary crossbraces. Any plant on this arbor will already have the illusion of height, so go ahead and give a slow grower a chance to climb.

Variation

TURQUOISE BLUE GABLE ARBOR

Design by
Antique Rose Emporium

Follow the principles in the Gable Arbor instructions and modify the measurements to fit your design. Extend the length of the posts. Sharpen the angle of the arches by attaching them further down on the posts. Add a decorative finial. Paint it any color in the rainbow, and lavish flowers on it!

ARTS AND CRAFTS ARBOR

Adapted Design by Olivier Rollin

Add a robust accent to any garden with this impressive Arts and Crafts-style arbor. We extended the side railings to the ground, creating trellis space to carry a profusion of flowers.

WHAT YOU NEED
Basic Tool Kit
Digging Kit
Additional Tools
- $3/32$" drill bit for piloting $2\frac{1}{2}$" deck screws
- $1/8$" drill bits for piloting $3\frac{1}{2}$" and 4" deck screws
- $1/4$" drill bit for piloting $3/8$" lag screws
- Jigsaw
- Circular saw (optional)

Materials and Supplies
- Thin, flexible strip of wood, roughly $3/8$" thick x 8' long
- Post ground braces
- Crossbraces

Hardware
- 1 lb. $2\frac{1}{2}$" deck screws
- 1 lb. $3\frac{1}{2}$" deck screws
- 8 lag screws, $4\frac{1}{2}$" long, with washers

CUTTING LIST

Code	Description	Qty.	Dimensions	Cut from
A	Crossbeams	2	$1\frac{1}{2}$" x $5\frac{1}{2}$" x 110"	2 pcs. 2 x 6 x 10'
B	Posts	4	$3\frac{1}{2}$" x $3\frac{1}{2}$" x 120"	4 pcs. 4 x 4 x 10'
C	Side Beams	2	$1\frac{1}{2}$" x $3\frac{1}{2}$" x $45\frac{1}{2}$"	2 pcs. 2 x 4 x 8'
D	Side Railings			
D-1	Rails	4	$1\frac{1}{2}$" x $3\frac{1}{2}$" x $38\frac{1}{2}$"	4 pcs. 2 x 4 x 8'
D-2	Pickets	14	$1\frac{1}{2}$" x $1\frac{1}{2}$" x 36"	14 pcs. ready made
E	Roof Pieces	3	$1\frac{1}{2}$" x $3\frac{1}{2}$" x 110"	3 pcs. 2 x 4 x 10'

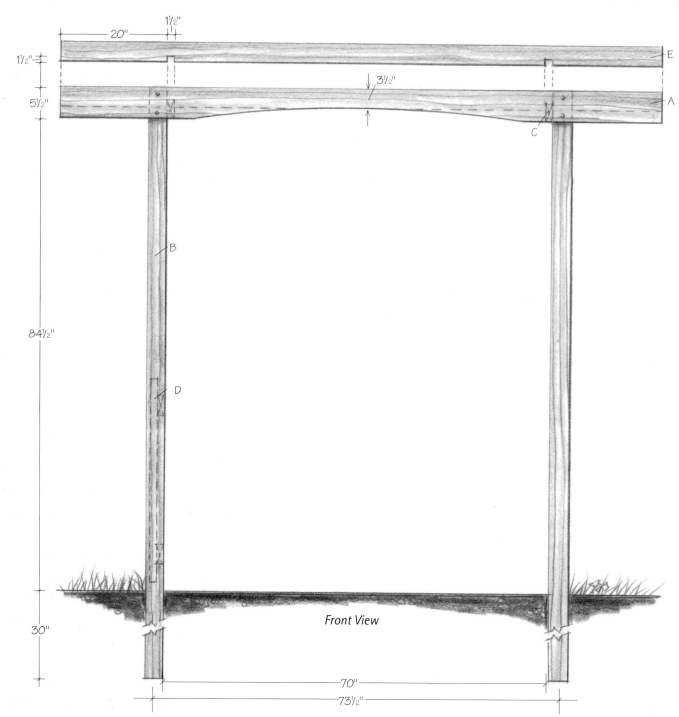

FIGURE 1:
Arts and Crafts Arbor

INSTRUCTIONS
Cutting the Pieces

1. Measure and cut the pieces according to the cutting list above. Lay out the dadoes on the roof pieces (E) as shown in figure 1, but don't cut them yet.

Shaping the Arcs on the Crossbeams

2. The crossbeams (A) have a gentle arc that gives this arbor a quiet simplicity. Because the radius of each arc is so long, use a strip of flexible wood instead of a

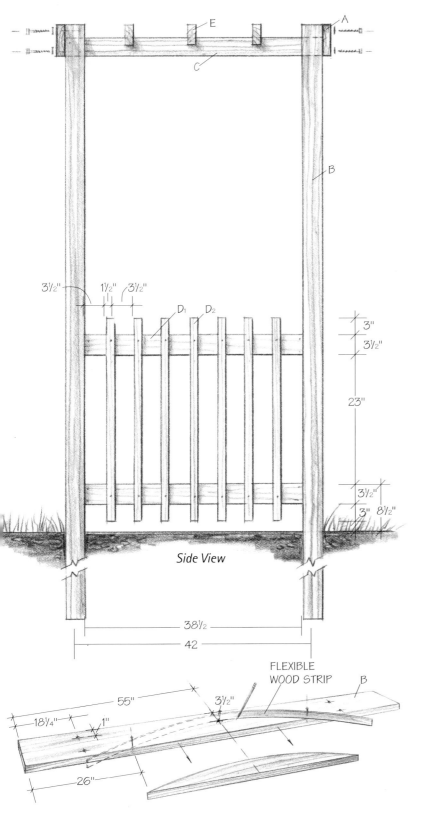

FIGURE 2: Laying Out the Arc

compass or trammel to lay out the curve, as shown in figure 2. Drive three screws partway into the 2 x 6 crossbeam stock, one at the beginning of the arc, one in the center, and one at the opposite end. The screws help position the strip for the next step.

3. Have your helper hold the flexible strip against the three screws on the stock. Pencil trace along the strip to draw the shape of the arc.

4. Use the dimensions in figure 2 to mark and drill four ¼" pilot holes for the lag screws on the crossbeam.

5. Repeat steps 2 to 4 for the second crossbeam.

6. With a jigsaw, cut out each arc.

Constructing the Post-and-Crossbeam Assemblies

7. Lay two posts (B) on the ground parallel to each other and 70" apart, with their top ends even, as shown in figure 1. Prop them up off the ground with 2 x 4 scraps. Lay a crossbeam over the posts with its top edge flush with the tops of the posts. Center the pilot holes you drilled in the crossbeam in step 4 on each post. Clamp the crossbeam to the posts with C-clamps. Use a carpenter's square and a tape measure to check that the posts are perpendicular with the beam, parallel to each other, and still 70" apart. With the ¼" bit, drill through the pilot holes and 2½" into the posts. Drive the lag screws to connect the crossbeam to the posts.

8. Attach temporary crossbraces to keep the posts in position. (See bracing information on page 28.)

9. Repeat steps 7 and 8 to construct the other post-and-crossbeam assembly.

Even a fence post can be a trellis for eager climbing flowers, such as clematis lanuginosa 'Candida'.

Setting the Post-and-Crossbeam Assemblies in the Ground

10. Call in your helpers. See Preparing the Site and Digging Postholes on page 00, and refer to project figure 1 for dimensions. Dig the holes for the posts.

11. With your helper, set both post-and-crossbeam assemblies in place into the postholes. Verify that the assemblies are plumb and aligned with each other, and the posts are 90" above ground. Hold them in place temporarily with ground post braces. (See bracing information on page 28.)

Installing the Side Beams

12. Have your helper hold one end of a side beam (C) in position and attach the opposite end to the inside of one of the posts with its end tight against the back of the crossbeam. Drill pilot holes through the side beam and drive 3½" screws through the side beam into the post. Nudge the opposite post-and-crossbeam assembly tight against the opposite end of the side beam and screw the side beam fast in the same manner as before.

13. Repeat step 12 to attach the second side beam.

Making and Installing the Side Railings

14. Each side railing (D) is assembled from two rails (D-1) and seven pickets (D-2). To build one railing, find a flat work surface and arrange two rails 23" apart and parallel with each other. Lay the pickets over the rails, spacing them 3½" apart and overhanging the rails by 3" at each end. (See figure 1, page 62.) If

necessary, use a piece of scrap 2 x 4 as a spacer block to help position the pickets accurately. Drill pilot holes through the pickets and drive 2½" screws through the holes and into the rails, checking for square.

15. Repeat step 14 to construct the second side railing.

16. Place one side railing between two of the posts so that the top of the bottom rail is 8½" above ground and both rails are flush with the posts on the inside of the arbor, as shown in figure 1. The pickets should face the outside of the arbor. Nudge the posts against the ends of the rails for a tight fit. Drill angled pilot holes through the ends of the rails and into the posts, and drive 3" screws to secure the railing. Repeat for the other side railing.

17. Check again that everything is straight and plumb, and backfill around the posts. Remove the temporary braces.

Installing the Roof Pieces

18. Check that the dado layout on the roof pieces (E) you drew in step 1 lines up with the tops of the side beams (C). Cut the dadoes, fit them over the side beams, and adjust if necessary. (Refer to the instructions on making dadoes on page 19.) Drill pilot holes and secure the roof pieces with 2½" screws driven at an angle through the roof pieces and into the side beams. Now that you've made an arbor in the popular Arts and Crafts tradition, should you make a few benches to set out in the garden nearby?

ROYAL BLUE ARCHES

Adapted Design by Olivier Rollin

These jaunty arches demand standup-and-salute colors. And as the photograph shows—the more the merrier! We jazzed up the design by using pairs of crosspieces over the entire arch. Making the arch is just a simple progression of cutting and gluing techniques. Once you've made one arch, you'll be a master arc builder!

It requires precise cutting to fit all the arch pieces together.

WHAT YOU NEED
Basic Tool Kit
Digging Kit
Additional Tools
- ³⁄₃₂" drill bit for piloting 1¼" and 2½" screws
- ⅛" drill bit for piloting 3" screw
- Power sander with rough sandpaper (optional)
- Belt sander with rough sanding belt (optional)
- Circular saw (optional)
- Stepladder, preferably two

Materials and Supplies
- Water-resistant wood glue
- 4 x 8' plywood work surface
- Temporary stretcher ties: 2 pcs. 2 x 4 x 2'
- Post ground braces
- Crossbraces

Hardware
- 1 lb. 1¼" deck screws
- 1 lb. 2½" deck screws
- 1 lb. 3" deck screws

CUTTING LIST

Code	Description	Qty.	Dimensions	Cut from
A	Arches	2		
A-1	Middle Gussets	2	½" x 3½" wide	A-1 & A-2:
A-2	Tenon Gussets	4	½" x 3½" wide	½" x 48 x 48½"
				exterior plywood
A-3	Half Arches	8	1½" x 3½" wide	2 pcs. 2 x 12 x 8'
B	Post	4	3½" x 3½" x 106"	4 pcs. 4 x 8 x 10'
C	Side Pieces	30	1½" x 1½" x 36"	30 pcs. 2 x 2 x 3'

Notes: The posts are standard 4 x 4s, which are sturdy and easy to find. The arches are layered to match the thickness of the posts.

The arches require precise cutting with the jigsaw: your cuts will be more accurate if you cut close to, but not on, the outside of the line. This will keep the line intact both while you're cutting it and later when you're sanding the curves smooth.

If you're using pressure treated wood, remember you can't paint until the wood has weathered, sometimes as long as a year. These arbors add such a spectacular touch to the garden, they're worth the wait. And you can enjoy their unpainted beauty in the meantime.

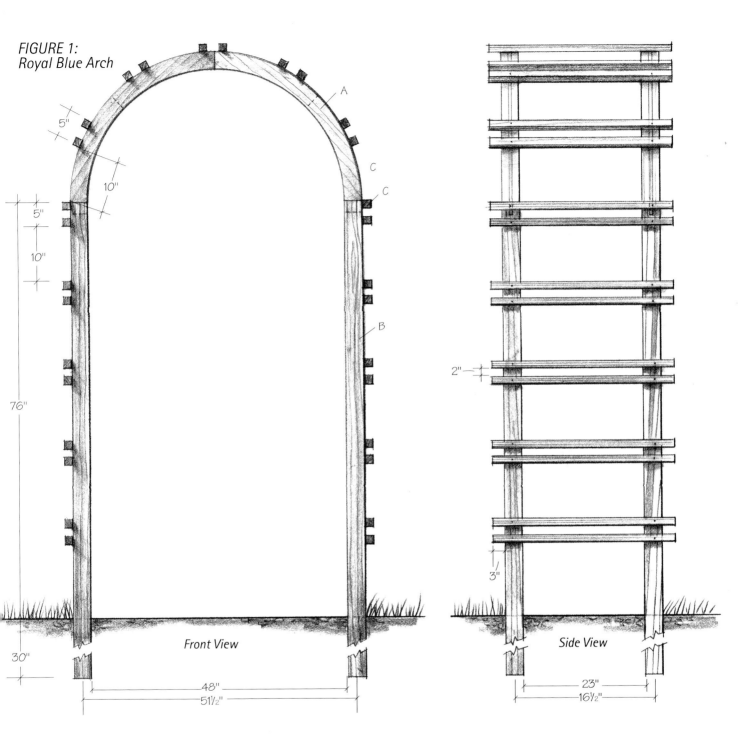

FIGURE 1:
Royal Blue Arch

5"

10"

5"

10"

76"

A

C

C

B

30"

Front View

48"

51½"

2"

3"

Side View

23"

16½"

INSTRUCTIONS *(for one arbor)*
Laying Out and Cutting the Arch Pieces

1. Refer to figure 1 to see how all the pieces will be assembled. Begin by making the plywood arch gussets (A-1 and A-2). The ½" plywood gussets will be sandwiched between layers of 1½" thick solid-wood arch pieces later for strength. Referring to figure 2 (on page 68), draw a vertical line (C-1 to C-2) on the ½" plywood, centering the line and making

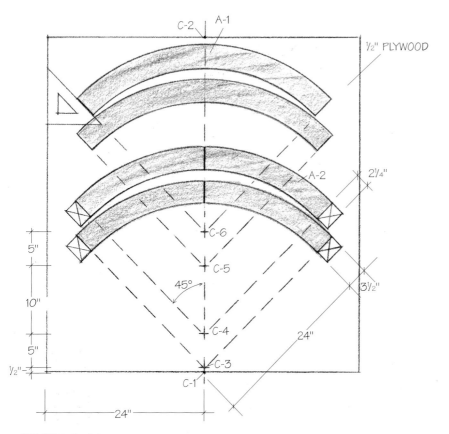

FIGURE 2: Arch Layout

sure it's parallel with the edges of the plywood. Mark the center of the arcs on the line so there are four centers (C-3, C-4, C-5 and C-6).

2. Use the drafting triangle to draw two lines at 45° angles from each of the four centerpoints, as represented by the dashed lines on figure 2. From each centerpoint, use a trammel to draw two concentric arcs for each of the four arcs. (See information on trammels and drawing arcs on page 16.) Adjust the trammel so the first arc has a 24" radius; the second arc has a radius of 27½".

3. The two lower sets of arcs on figure 2 will be cut in half at the centerline later to make the four tenon gussets (A-2). These two arcs require a little more drafting work. At both ends of each arc,

lay out a 2¼" long tenon, using the drafting square and the dimensions on figure 2.

4. Once you've completed the plywood arch layouts, cut along the lines with the jigsaw. Remember to cut the lower two arcs in half to create four tenon gussets (A-2). Choose one of the middle gussets (A-1), the one on which you did the best cutting job, to use as a template for laying out the half arches (A-3). Set the remaining gussets aside.

5. Position the middle gusset (A-1) onto the 2 x 12 stock to lay out the half-arches (A-3). Use a pencil to trace around the gusset, moving the gusset and re-tracing until you've drawn eight half arches on the stock. Carefully saw along the lines with the jigsaw to cut out the eight arches.

Preparing the Work Surface

6. In this step, you'll draw the arch on a 4 x 8 plywood work surface to use as a guide when assembling the arch pieces. Trace a horizontal line across the plywood sheet 27½" away from the top 48" edge, and mark its centerline. With the trammel set to the 27½" radius, pivot the trammel on the centerline to draw an arc on the plywood. Don't worry that the lower ends of the arc extend past the edges of the plywood.

Fitting the Arch Pieces

7. Refer to figure 3 to see how the two arches are assembled. Each arch is composed of three layers: one middle layer made from the plywood gussets (A-1 and

A-2), sandwiched between two outer layers made from the solid wood half arches (A-3). The middle layer extends beyond the bottom of the arch to form tenons. You'll need to dry-assemble the pieces before you glue them to make sure everything fits. Position two half arches (A-3) such that their top edges align with the arc you drew on the work surface in step 6. The half arches butt together at the top of the arch, and their bottom edges extend past the edges of the plywood at the point where you drew the horizontal line in step 6.

8. Place the middle gusset (A-1) on top of the half-arches, aligning it such that it straddles the center of the joints where the two half-arches meet. To complete the middle layer, position the two tenon gussets (A-2) on either side of the middle gusset. Make sure the tenons extend 2¼" beyond the two half arches, as shown in figure 3.

9. Complete the dry assembly by placing the two remaining half arches (A-3) on top of the plywood gussets. Verify that the bottoms of all the four half arches are aligned with each other to ensure you'll have a square joint with the top of the posts later. Make any necessary adjustments.

Positioning Pilot Holes and Screws

10. Remove the two top half-arches (A-3) from the assembly and set them aside. Then secure the two remaining layers to the plywood with C-clamps, making sure all the parts are still aligned properly.

11. Center pilot holes 2" from the ends

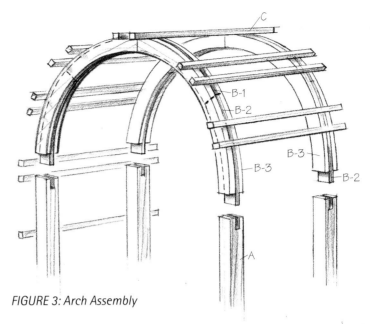

FIGURE 3: Arch Assembly

of the middle layer gusset pieces. Drill pilot holes through the pieces and drive 2" screws through the holes into the bottom two half-arches. Remove the C-clamps.

12. Pick up the top pieces and place them back on top of the middle layer. Align and clamp all the pieces to the plywood. On the top pieces, drill pilot holes as you did in the previous step, but don't drive in the screws yet.

13. Remove the C-clamps, pick up the top pieces and drive 2" screws through the pilot holes so that they extend ¼" on the back sides of the pieces. Set the pieces aside.

14. Back up the 2" screws in the middle layer to free the pieces and again drive the screws so that they extend ¼" from the backs of the pieces. Pick them up and back the screws in so that they extend ¼" from the backs of the pieces. Keep the bottom layer of the arch on the plywood.

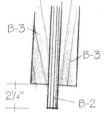

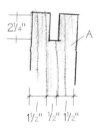

Tenon Detail

Because the arbor is so airy, its bright color works well with equally vibrant flowers.

Assembling the Arch Pieces

15. Spread glue on all the adjoining surfaces. (This means that the gusset pieces in the middle will have glue on both sides. Do not put any glue on the tenon parts of these pieces yet.)

16. Starting with the middle layer, reposition it onto the bottom layer by aligning the protruding screws with the pilot holes below them. Drive the 2" screws all the way through the pieces to hold them in place. Next, reposition and align the top layer and drive the 3" screws through the pilot holes to secure all three layers. Drive additional 3" screws alongside the positioning screws to secure the three layers together.

17. Clean off the glue that oozed out when you drove in the screws. Use a rag or piece of wood to scrape the glue off the sides of arch and the tenons, as well as the plywood surface. Set the arch aside on a flat surface.

18. Repeat steps 7 through 17 for the second arch.

19. Stack both arches on the flat surface. Weigh them down with rocks or concrete blocks until the glue is set, at least overnight.

20. Since you're probably going to paint this project later on when the glue is completely set, sand the sides of the arches smooth now, but don't round the edges. Use the wood rasp, or a belt sander and/or power sander. Wear a protective mask when you're sanding pressure treated lumber.

21. When you have smoothed out the curves, finish sanding with fine sandpaper. In the same way, smooth the front face of the arch, which is the side that doesn't have any screws in it.

Making the Dado Cuts on Top of the Four Posts

22. Refer to the section on dado cuts on page 19, and to figure 3 for the specific dimensions for this project. With the square, make sure that the end of the post you're working is square and true. Draw the lines for the dado cuts on the posts. Make the cuts with the handsaw and chisel. When the dado cuts are finished, cut the posts to 106" long.

Assembling the Post-and-Arch Units

23. Place one of the arches on top of the plywood work surface. Align it with the lines you drew in step 6, and secure it to the plywood with C-clamps. Place one post alongside the plywood and add spacer blocks under it so it is even with the plywood. Insert the tenon of the arch into the dado cuts of the posts and check for fit. With the chisel, make the necessary adjustments at this point.

24. When satisfied with the fit, spread glue on the surfaces of the joints and insert the tenon into the top of the post, keeping the post aligned with the edge of the plywood. Secure the joint with 3" screws.

25. Repeat steps 23 and 24 for the other post.

26. Refer to the temporary crossbracing information on page 28. Add temporary crossbraces to the two posts. Cut the ends of braces flush with the posts so they won't be in the way later on when you attach the side pieces to the sides of the posts. You have completed one post-and-arch unit.

27. Repeat steps 23 to 26 for the other post-and-arch unit.

Assembling the Arbor

28. Position the two units on the ground, as shown on figure 4. To keep them the right distance apart from each other, cut five long stretcher ties 23" in length from scrap 2 x 4s. Make sure that both arches are aligned with each other, then temporarily attach the ties to the arch units with 2½" screws, as shown in figure 4.

29. Once the two units are temporarily attached to each other, you'll screw the side pieces onto them. Refer to figure 1 for dimensions, and mark the positions of the side pieces on the posts and arches. Make a 3" thick spacer block by attaching two pieces of 2 x 4 scrap together and use it to keep the ends of the side pieces aligned 3" away from the side of the arbor. Position the side pieces on the marks. Drill pilot holes 5" from the ends of each side piece, then drive 2½" screws through the holes into the sides of the arbor. Take down the stretcher ties. You have now completed the arbor.

Preparing the Site and Digging the Holes

30. Call in your helpers. See Preparing the Site (page 23) and Digging Postholes (page 26), and refer to project figure 1 on page 67 for dimensions. Dig the holes for the posts.

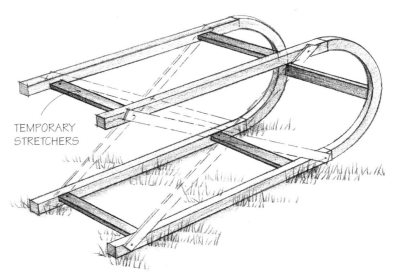

TEMPORARY STRETCHERS

FIGURE 4: Arch-and-Post Assembly

Installing the Arbor

31. Stand the arbor on its legs and place it into the postholes. Make sure it is plumb before backfilling around the posts and removing the temporary cross-braces.

32. If you're using pressure treated wood, you know you have to let the wood weather for at least at least six months (or more) before you can paint it. If you're using regular untreated wood, preserve or paint it right away. By the way, whoever said you had to paint an arbor all one color? Go crazy with color if you want!

GRAND GATEWAY ARBOR

Adapted Design by Olivier Rollin

With its rounded arches and regal lines, this arbor stands as a grand gateway between two levels of the garden. We simplified the design to incorporate easy-to-find lengths of pressure treated lumber and stylish store-bought finials.

WHAT YOU NEED

Basic Tool Kit

Digging Kit

Additional Tools

- ⌁ ³/₃₂" drill bit for piloting 1¼" and 2½" deck screws
- ⌁ ⅛" drill bit for piloting 3" deck screws
- ⌁ ¼" drill bit for piloting ⅜" lag screws
- ⌁ Jigsaw
- ⌁ Circular saw (optional)
- ⌁ Miter saw (optional)

Materials and Supplies

- ⌁ Water-resistant wood glue
- ⌁ 2 scrap wood spacer blocks, 5½" long
- ⌁ 1 scrap 2 x 4, 1' long
- ⌁ 1 sheet of ¾" x 4' x 8' plywood or similar work surface
- ⌁ Post ground braces
- ⌁ Crossbraces

Hardware

- ⌁ 1 lb. 1¼" deck screws
- ⌁ 1 lb. 2½" deck screws
- ⌁ 1 lb. 3" deck screws
- ⌁ 8 lag bolts, ⅜" x 4" with washers

CUTTING LIST

Code	Description	Qty.	Dimensions	Cut from
A	Side Lattice Panels	2		
A-1	Uprights	6	¾" x 1½" x 84"	6 pcs. 1 x 2 x 8'
A-2	Crosspieces	22	¾" x 1½" x 31½"	6 pcs. 1 x 2 x 8'
B	Arches	2		
B-1		2	1½" x 11¼" x 59¾"	1 pc. 2 x 12 x 10'
B-1		2	1½" x 5½" x 59¾"	1 pc. 2 x 6 x 10'
C	Decorative Arch Frames	2		
C-1	Bottom Pieces	2	¾" x 1½" x 42½"	1 pc. 2 x 2 x 8'
C-2	Centerpieces	4	¾" x 1½ x 11"	1 pc. 1 x 2 x 1'
C-3	Side pieces	2	¾" x 1" x 11"	1 pc. 1 x 2 x 1'
D	Posts	4	3½" x 3½" x 107"	4 pcs. 4 x 4 x 10'
E	Side Braces	2	1½" x 3½" x 35"	1 pc. 2 x 4 x 8'
F	Roof Pieces	2	1½" x 3½" x 35"	1 pc. 2 x 4 x 8'
G	Finials	4		Ready made, with lag bolts

INSTRUCTIONS
Cutting the Pieces

1. Refer to figure 1 for overall lay-out of the project. Measure and cut the pieces according to the cutting list. The side pieces (C-3) have a 22° angle cut at one end, as shown in figure 4. Cut the stock for the arches to the dimensions shown; you'll work on it later to complete the curved arches.

FIGURE 1:
Grand Gateway Arbor

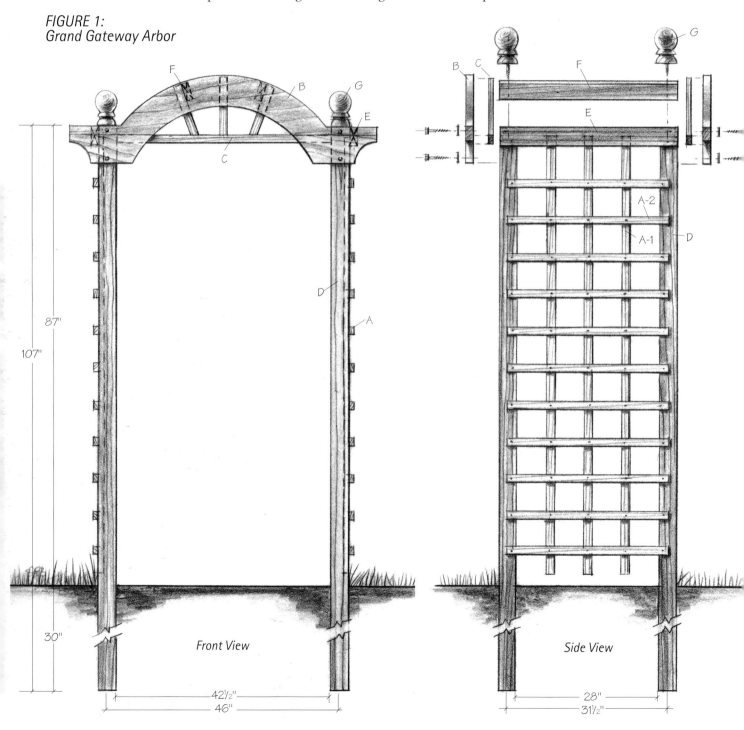

Front View

Side View

Making the Two Side Lattice Panels

2. You'll assemble all 28 pieces of the two side lattice panels (A) and later screw the panels to the sides of the arbor. Work on one panel at a time. On the plywood, lay out 11 lattice crosspieces (A-2), 5½" apart. See figure 2 to guide you. Use the 5½" blocks of scrap wood as spacers to help position the pieces evenly, and use the straightedge and the framing square to align and straighten them. To keep the crosspieces in place as you work, drill pilot holes 1" from their ends, then drive 1¼" screws through the crosspieces and partially into the plywood as you go. You'll use the same holes to attach the lattice panels to the posts later.

3. Measure and mark 13½" from the ends of the top and bottom crosspieces to position one edge of the upright lattice piece (A-1). Place the upright piece on the marks so that one end extends 8" beyond the top crosspiece. Drill pilot holes and use 1¼" screws to attach the upright to each crosspiece. Use the 5½" spacer blocks to align the remaining two upright pieces on either side of the centered one, making sure the tops of these uprights overhang 8" the top crosspiece. Attach the two uprights to the crosspieces with 1¼" screws. Set the assembled panel aside.

4. Repeat steps 2 and 3 to make the second side lattice panel and set it aside, too.

Making the Arch Stock

5. There are two arches (B). To make them, you'll assemble the pieces in pairs

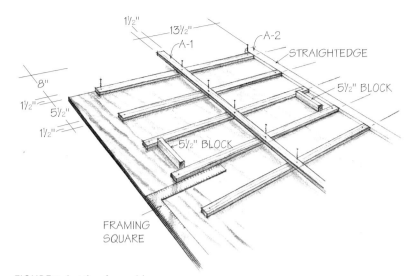

FIGURE 2: Lattice Assembly

and glue them together. Each arch (B) needs to be cut from a 16¾" wide board, which you'll make by edge-gluing two pieces of lumber (B-1 and B-2). Spread an even coat of glue on one edge of each piece, then use the 24" bar clamps to assemble the pieces. When the glue has dried, take one of the edge-glued boards and lay it on the worksurface.

6. Each arch has an outside radius of 26". Since the centerpoint for the radius falls outside the arch stock, you need to add a temporary piece of scrap wood to widen the stock in preparation for

A wide, landscaped ascent complements a majestic arbor, especially one with a complicated design.

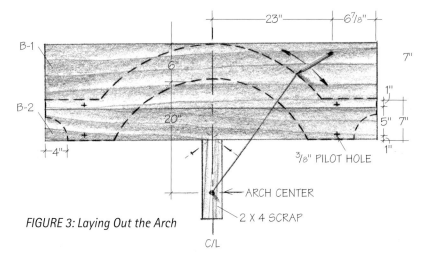

FIGURE 3: Laying Out the Arch

drawing the arc. As shown in figure 3, toenail a piece of 2 x 4 scrap wood in the center of the long side of the arch stock and trace a centerline through the scrap piece and across the stock.

7. With the trammel (see information on page 16), trace the two arcs of the arch. The outer top arc has a radius of 26"; the inner arc is 20".

8. Lay out the remainder of the arch, as shown in figure 3. Use the compass to draw the 4" radius at each end of the arch. Mark and drill four ¼" pilot holes for the lag screws.

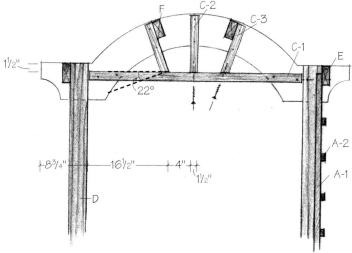

FIGURE 4: Arch Detail

9. Saw to your layout lines with the jigsaw.

10. Repeat steps 5 through 9 to create the second arch.

Making the Decorative Arch Frame

11. Refer to figure 4 to identify the four pieces on each decorative frame (C-1 and C-2, and two C-3 pieces) and to see how they are laid out. Position the centerpiece (C-2) at the middle of the bottom piece (C-1). Drill a pilot hole through the bottom piece and drive a 3" screw to attach both pieces.

12. Position the side pieces (C-3) 4" from the centerpiece. As before, drill pilot holes and attach them to the bottom piece with 3" screws.

13. Repeat steps 11 and 12 for the second decorative frame. Set both frames aside.

Completing the Arches

14. To finish the arches, screw the two decorative arch frames (C) in place (see figure 4). Carefully position each frame centered on the back side of its corresponding arch, drill pilot holes through the frame members, and drive 1¼" screws through the holes and into the arch. Set both completed arches aside.

Making and Installing the Post-and-Arch Assembly

15. Construct one post-and-arch assembly at a time. Start by laying a pair of posts (D) on a level spot on the ground, parallel to each other. Lay one arch (B) on top of the posts, with its decorative frame facing the ground. Align the top straight edges of the arch with the top of the posts, as shown in figure 4. Next, move both posts against the ends of the bottom frame piece (C-1) and use C-clamps to temporarily clamp the posts to the arch.

16. With the framing square, make sure that the posts are perpendicular to the arch. Also, measure $42\frac{1}{2}$" between the posts at their bottom ends to make sure they're parallel to each other.

17. Use the pilot holes you drilled in the arches as guides to drill $\frac{1}{4}$" holes into the posts. Then drive the four lag screws, adding washers, to connect the arch to the posts.

18. Attach the temporary post braces to the post-and-arch assembly with $1\frac{1}{4}$" screws. (See Bracing on page 28.)

19. Repeat steps 15 through 18 to construct the second post-and-arch assembly.

20. Call in your helpers. See Preparing the Site and Digging Postholes on page 23 and refer to this project's figure 1 for dimensions. Dig the holes for the posts.

21. Install one post-and-arch assembly in two postholes so that the tops of the posts are 87" above ground. With the level, check that the assembly is plumb. Install the temporary ground post braces. Place the braces on the inside of the posts, underneath the arches, so the braces will be out of the way when you attach the side panels.

22. Repeat step 21 for the second post-and-arch assembly. Make sure that it is aligned and level with the first unit, and 28" apart from it. Temporarily brace the second assembly as you did the first.

Attaching the Side Braces and Roof Pieces

23. Standing on the stepladder, attach the two side braces (E) to the sides of the posts (B) with $2\frac{1}{2}$" screws, as shown in figure 1. Nudge in the post-and-arch assemblies to get a tight fit against the ends of the braces.

24. Next, secure the roof pieces (F) to the back of the arch by driving $2\frac{1}{2}$" screws at an angle through the pieces and into the framework of the arches.

Attaching the Lattice Panels and Finials

25. To position the lattice panels (A) on the sides of the arbor (see fig. 1), hold them in place temporarily with C-clamps. Drive $1\frac{1}{4}$" screws through the pilot holes you made in step 2 to attach the panels to the posts. Attach the upper ends of the three upright pieces to the back of the side braces (E) with $1\frac{1}{4}$" screws, as shown in figure 1.

26. Make a last check with the level to make sure that the structure is plumb. Backfill around the posts and remove all the temporary braces.

27. To put the finishing touches on the arch, drill pilot holes for lag screws in the tops of the four posts, and attach the four finials. Walk up, walk down, walk through, walk around—enjoy your work from all its wonderful perspectives.

The brilliant lavender flowers of the Blue Ravine Clematis offer double performances— they bloom in spring and again in summer.

LASTING LEGACY ARBOR

Adapted Design by Olivier Rollin

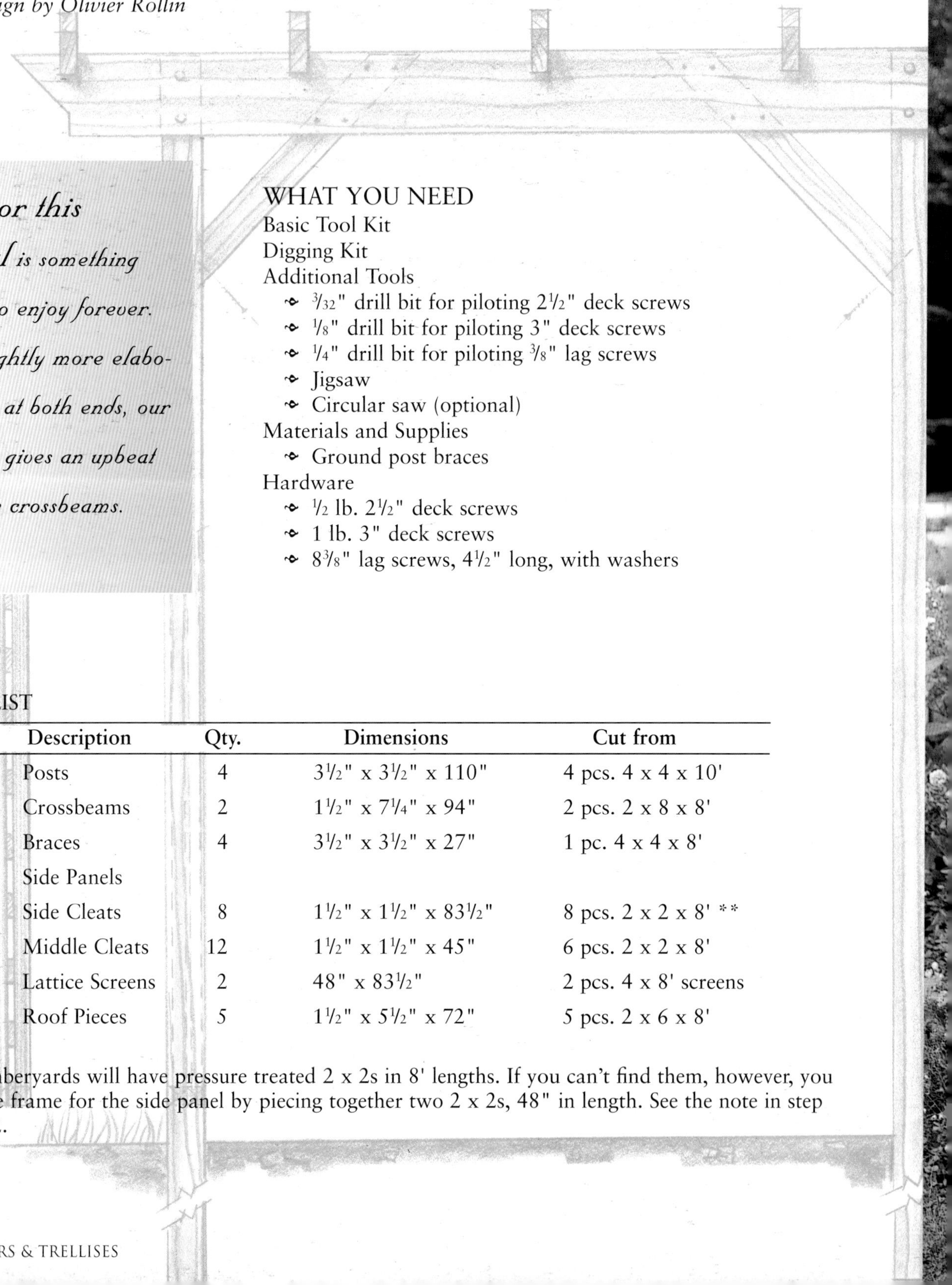

An arbor this beautiful is something you want to enjoy forever. With a slightly more elaborate angle at both ends, our adaptation gives an upbeat look to the crossbeams.

WHAT YOU NEED

Basic Tool Kit
Digging Kit
Additional Tools
- $^3/_{32}$" drill bit for piloting $2^1/_2$" deck screws
- $^1/_8$" drill bit for piloting 3" deck screws
- $^1/_4$" drill bit for piloting $^3/_8$" lag screws
- Jigsaw
- Circular saw (optional)

Materials and Supplies
- Ground post braces

Hardware
- $^1/_2$ lb. $2^1/_2$" deck screws
- 1 lb. 3" deck screws
- 8 $^3/_8$" lag screws, $4^1/_2$" long, with washers

CUTTING LIST

Code	Description	Qty.	Dimensions	Cut from
A	Posts	4	$3^1/_2$" x $3^1/_2$" x 110"	4 pcs. 4 x 4 x 10'
B	Crossbeams	2	$1^1/_2$" x $7^1/_4$" x 94"	2 pcs. 2 x 8 x 8'
C	Braces	4	$3^1/_2$" x $3^1/_2$" x 27"	1 pc. 4 x 4 x 8'
D	Side Panels			
D1	Side Cleats	8	$1^1/_2$" x $1^1/_2$" x $83^1/_2$"	8 pcs. 2 x 2 x 8' **
D2	Middle Cleats	12	$1^1/_2$" x $1^1/_2$" x 45"	6 pcs. 2 x 2 x 8'
D-3	Lattice Screens	2	48" x $83^1/_2$"	2 pcs. 4 x 8' screens
E	Roof Pieces	5	$1^1/_2$" x $5^1/_2$" x 72"	5 pcs. 2 x 6 x 8'

** Some lumberyards will have pressure treated 2 x 2s in 8' lengths. If you can't find them, however, you can make the frame for the side panel by piecing together two 2 x 2s, 48" in length. See the note in step 6 on page 82.

INSTRUCTIONS
Cutting the Pieces

1. Refer to the cutting list to cut all the pieces to length. Use a jigsaw to make the 45° angle cuts and the 90° shoulder cuts on the ends of the crossbeams (B) and the 45° angles on the roof pieces (E). Lay out the lines for the dado cuts on the roof pieces but don't cut them out yet. With a ¼" bit, drill two pilot holes on the crossbeams 14½" from each end of the beams, as shown in figure 1.

FIGURE 1:
Lasting Legacy Arbor

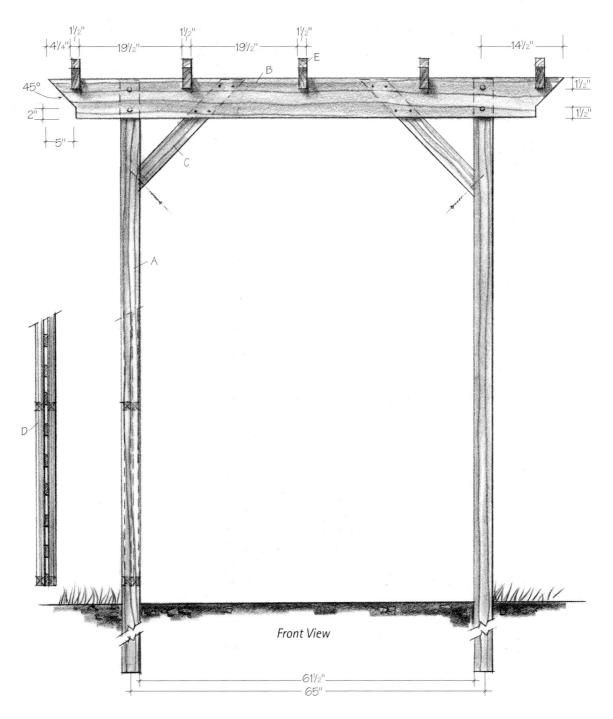

Front View

Building the Post-and-Beam Assemblies

2. Construct one post-and-beam assembly at a time. Place two posts (A) on the ground, 61½" apart, parallel to each other with their ends lined up. Space the posts off the ground with scrap 2 x 4s. Refer to figure 1 and place one cross-beam (B) on top of the posts, even with their top ends. Check with a tape measure and a carpenter's square that the

The exquisite antique rose, Rosette Delizy, gives elegance to any arbor.

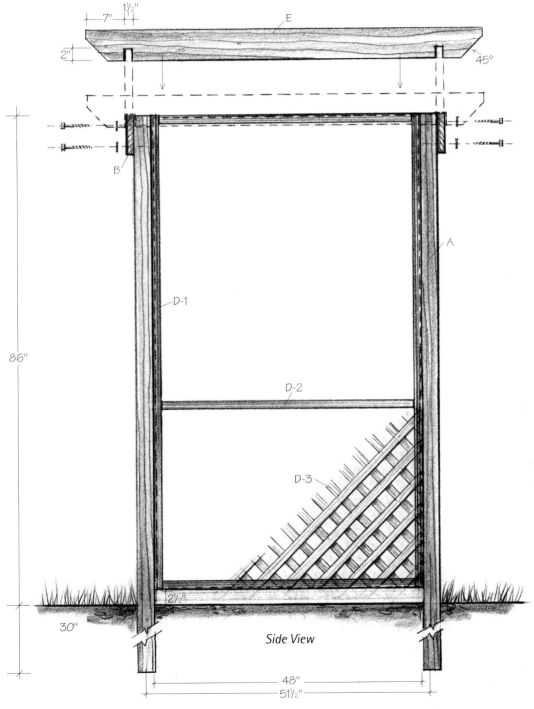

Side View

posts are correctly spaced apart and perpendicular to the crossbeam. Temporarily clamp the crossbeam to the post with C-clamps. With the ¼" bit, drill through the pilot holes in the crossbeam and into the posts. Install the lag screws and washers to connect the assembly.

3. Call in your helper. Turn the assembly over lengthwise, taking care not to stress its joints. Use a carpenter's square and a tape measure to make sure that the three pieces are still square to each other. Position one brace (C), as shown in figure 1, with one end even with the top of the crossbeam and the other flush with the faces of a post. Clamp the brace to the crossbeam with two C-clamps. Drill four ⅛" pilot holes through the brace and into the crossbeam. Drive 3" screws to secure this joint.

4. Drill two ⅛" pilot holes through the brace and into the post. Position these holes 2½" apart and about 2" from the end of the brace. Drive 3" screws, making sure that the brace doesn't slide along the post as you do so. Remove the clamps and use them

to position and fasten the other brace to complete the first post-and-beam assembly.

5. Repeat steps 2 through 4 for the second post-and-beam assembly.

Assembling the Side Panels

6. Each side panel is comprised of one lattice screen (D-3) sandwiched between two frames (D, D-1, and D-2), as shown in figure 2. Start by assembling one frame, which consists of two side cleats (D-1) and three middle cleats (D-2). Refer to figure 2. To hold the frame joints in position while you're working on them, clamp a scrap piece of plywood over each joint until you've driven the screw to secure the joint. Drill a pilot hole and drive a 3" screw through the hole to secure the joints.

Note: If you have to use two 2 x 2 x 4' pieces instead of one 2 x 2 x 8' to make the side cleats (D-1), trim half of the 4' pieces to 35½". You'll need to stagger the joints of the lower frame with those of the upper frame, as shown in figure 2. Then drive two 3" screws through the overlapping sections when assembling the frames and the lattice screen together in step 8.

7. Repeat step 6 to construct the remaining three frames.

8. Next, you'll assemble the frames with the lattice screens (D-3). Make one panel at a time. Place one of the lattice screens on one of the assembled frames, as shown in figure 2. Then place another frame on top, sandwiching the lattice

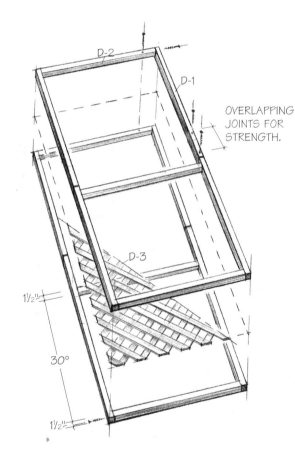

FIGURE 2: Side Panel Assembly

screen between the two frames. Use C-clamps to hold the three pieces in position, drill ⅛" pilot holes, and drive 3" screws to make the assembly permanent. Make sure to position the screws where the two layers of the lattice cross.

9. Repeat steps 6 through 8 for the other panel.

Installing the Post-and-Beam Assemblies and Attaching the Side Panels

10. Call in your helper again. See Preparing the Site (page 23) and Digging Postholes (page 26) and refer to this project figure 1 on page 81 for dimensions. Dig the holes for the posts.

11. Position the two post-and-beam assemblies in the postholes. Make sure they are aligned with each other, and the tops of the post and the crossbeams are 86" above ground.

12. Position one of the side panels between the posts on one side of the arbor. Align it flush with the tops of the posts and center it with the sides of the posts. Hold the panel in place with C-clamps and secure it to the posts with 3" screws driven though ⅛" pilot holes. Repeat for the other side panel.

13. Check one more time that the structure is plumb and level and backfill around the posts.

Installing the Roof Pieces

14. Verify that the dado layout on the roof pieces (E) you drew in step 1 line up with the tops of the crossbeams (B). Cut the dadoes, try them on the crossbeams, and adjust if necessary. (Refer to the instructions on making dado cuts, page 19.) Drill pilot holes and secure the roof pieces with 2½" deck screws driven at an angle through the roof pieces and into the crossbeams. An arbor this beautiful will definitely attract visitors, so consider planting aromatic roses or jasmine to add to their enjoyment.

One of the most appealing things about arbors painted white is how wonderful they look when surrounded by snow.

POET'S ARBOR

Adapted Design by Olivier Rollin

WHAT YOU NEED

Basic Tool Kit
Digging Kit
Additional Tools
- Heavy objects to weigh down your work
- Bench vise
- $\frac{1}{8}$" drill bit for piloting 3" deck screws
- $\frac{3}{32}$" drill bit for piloting $1\frac{1}{4}$" and 2" deck screws
- Jigsaw
- Table saw or miter saw

Materials and Supplies
- 100-grit sandpaper
- Thumbtacks
- Weather-resistant wood glue
- 1 sheet $\frac{3}{4}$" x 4" x 8" plywood
- 2 pieces posterboard, 28" x 44"
- Post ground braces

Hardware
- 2 lbs. $1\frac{1}{4}$" deck screws
- 3 lbs. 2" deck screws
- 3 lbs. 3" deck screws

It's as beautiful as a lyric poem and needs an abundant setting to match its majestic size. Although this project is best suited for an experienced woodworker, a beginner with time and patience can successfully build it.

CUTTING LIST

Code	Description	Qty.	Dimensions	Cut from
A	Arches	3		
A-1	Curved Front Pieces	6	$\frac{3}{4}$" x $8\frac{1}{2}$" x 34"	1 pc. 1 x 10 x 8'
A-2	Gussets	3	$\frac{3}{4}$" x $8\frac{1}{2}$" x $30\frac{1}{2}$"	1 pc. 1 x 10 x 10'
A-3	Trim Pieces	6	$\frac{3}{4}$" x $5\frac{3}{4}$" x 13"	1 pc.1 x 8 x 8'
A-4	Short Rafters	6	$\frac{3}{4}$" x $5\frac{1}{2}$" x $22\frac{1}{2}$"	1 pc.1 x 6 x 10'
A-5	Long Rafters	6	$\frac{3}{4}$" x $5\frac{1}{2}$" x 31"	1 pc. 1 x 6 x 8'
B	Decorative Chevrons	88	$1\frac{1}{2}$" x $3\frac{1}{2}$" x 7"	8 pcs. 2 x 4 x 8'
C	Posts	8	$3\frac{1}{2}$" x $3\frac{1}{2}$" x 110"	8 pcs. 4 x 4 x 10'
D	Beams	4	$1\frac{1}{2}$" x $3\frac{1}{2}$" x 50"	2 pcs. 2 x 4 x 10'
E	Side Pieces	20	$1\frac{1}{2}$" x $3\frac{1}{2}$" x 50"	10 pcs. 2 x 4 x 10'
F	Roof Pieces	16	$\frac{3}{4}$" x $3\frac{1}{2}$" x 67"	16 pcs. 81 x 4 x 12'

Note: This project is made from many parts. Instead of cutting all the pieces before assembly, cut as you go as we've indicated in the instructions.

Tip: When you make scrolling cuts in a thick piece of wood with a jigsaw, and then use that piece as a template for sub-

sequent pieces, you risk duplicating any errors and imperfections that occur during cutting. Using thinner and easier-to-cut posterboard for templates, as we did in this project, ensures more accuracy, which is essential to achieve the elegant curve of the arch.

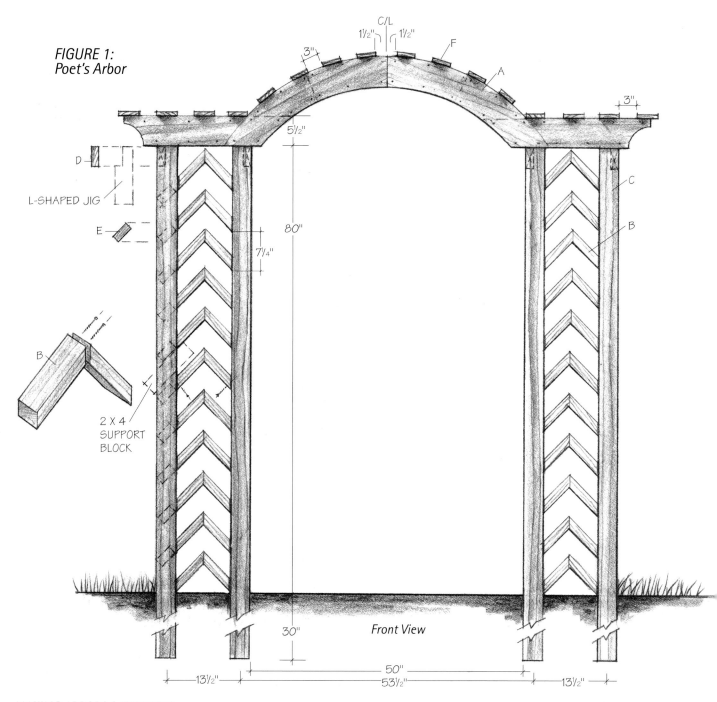

FIGURE 1:
Poet's Arbor

INSTRUCTIONS
Making the First Template

1. Each arch for this project is made from nine pieces of wood stacked, or laminated together, as shown in figure 6 page 89. To help with the arch construction, you'll need a total of five poster-board templates. Three templates define the curved area of the arch; the remaining two templates help with constructing the straight sections. Refer to figure 2 on page 88 to make the first curved template (A-1). Start by taping the two pieces of posterboard together along their 44" sides to get a surface area that measures 44" x 56".

The sturdy Poet's Arbor would give a vigorous climber like the flashy Tahitian Dawn Bougainvillea the support it needs.

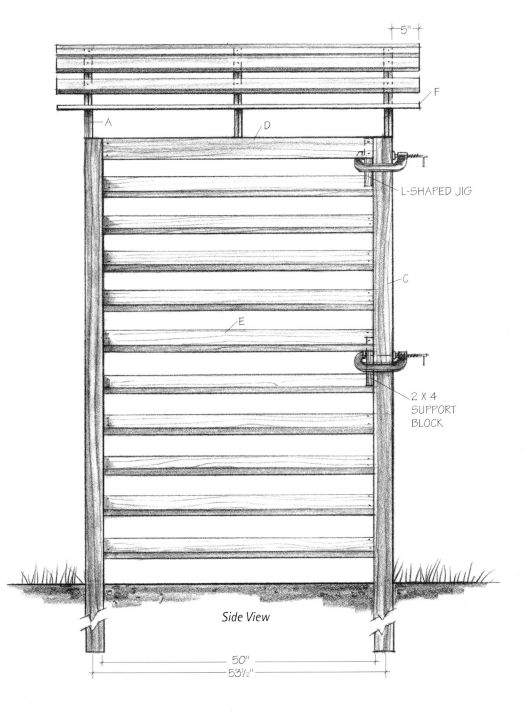

Side View

2. Turn the taped-together posterboard vertical. Using the straightedge and pencil, draw a line parallel to and ¹/₂" inside the right edge of the posterboard. (See fig. 2.) Mark the reference points, C, C-1, C-2, C-3, and C-4 on the vertical line. Leave at least 12" below point C because you'll use the remainder of the posterboard later.

3. Draw horizontal lines across the board from points C-3 and C-4.

4. Using the trammel (see information on page 16), draw two arcs at the points where the centerpoint C intersects at both C-1 and C-2. Both arcs start from the vertical line and end on the lower horizontal line, as shown in figure 2.

5. The lower horizontal line and the lower arc intersect at point C-5. Draw a line between C and C-5 and extend it

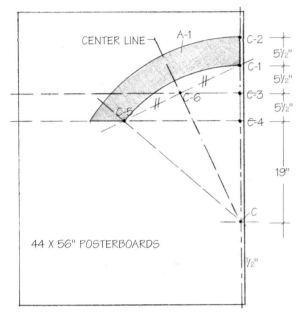

FIGURE 2: Curved Template A-1

across the arc lines. Draw another line between point C-5 and C-1. Measure and mark the middle of that line at C-6. Draw another line, the centerline, between C and C-6, also extending it across the arc lines.

6. With a utility knife, carefully cut out the template A-1, shown shaded in figure 2. Later, you'll create two more curved templates by modifying template A-1.

Making the Two Straight Templates

7. From the remaining bottom portion of the posterboard, cut two strips, 5¹/₂" x 44". To create the straight template for the short rafters (A-4), place template A-1 22¹/₂" from the top left side of one of the strips. (See fig. 3.) Trace the bottom left side of A-1 onto the strip. With a compass set to a 4" radius, draw a quarter-circle on the bottom left of the strip.

8. To make the second template for the long rafters (A-5), use the same template A-1; position it the same manner, 22¹/₂" from the left of the other strip. This time trace the right side of the arc onto the strip. Draw the same quarter-circle with a 4" radius on the bottom left.

9. With the utility knife cut out both templates and set them aside.

Making the Curved Front Pieces

10. You'll need two curved front pieces (A-1) per arch, for a total of six pieces. You'll use template A-1 to lay out the curves on the stock. With a sharp pencil, trace the edges of the template A-1 six times onto the 1 x 10 lumber. Use two thumbtacks to hold the posterboard onto

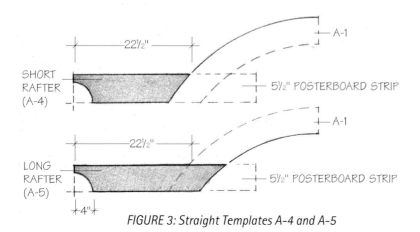

FIGURE 3: Straight Templates A-4 and A-5

the stock. Set aside the template for use later.

11. With the jigsaw, cut out the six front pieces you just traced onto the lumber. Set them aside.

Making the Gusset Pieces

12. To make the three gusset pieces (A-2), you need to modify template A-1 into template A-2. As shown in figure 4, cut off the bottom part of A-1 with the utility knife. Two marked lines will remain on the template; you'll use those lines later to make template A-3.

13. With the new template A-2, trace a total of three gusset pieces on the 1 x 10 lumber. Remember to transfer in the tracing the centerline you drew on the middle of the template in step 5.

14. With the jigsaw, cut the three gusset pieces you just traced. Set them aside.

Making the Six Trim Pieces

15. To create the template for the trim pieces (A-3), cut along the two lines left on template A-2, retaining the middle section, as shown in figure 5. Now that you've modified the template to become template A-3, use it to trace the six trim pieces onto the 1 x 8 lumber.

16. With the jigsaw, cut the six trim pieces and set them aside.

Making the Rafter Pieces

17. Using template A-4, trace six short rafters (A-4) onto the 1 x 6 lumber and cut out the parts with the jigsaw. Then trace and cut the six long rafters (A-5) onto the 1 x 6 stock, using template A-5. Set all 12 pieces aside.

Assembling the Arches

18. To make assembling the arches easy and accurate, you'll need to first make a jig from the sheet of plywood, as shown in figure 6. To construct the jig, first place a straightedge flush with the bottom edge of the plywood and draw a line on the plywood, following the top edge of the straightedge. Temporarily remove the straightedge, and, starting from the line you drew, draw the outline of the arch onto the plywood, as shown in figure 6. Use the trammel set at the same two radii you used in step 4 to draw the outer and inner arcs. To position the trammel point accurately, temporarily attach a piece of scrap 1 x 4 at the bottom of the plywood sheet, using the

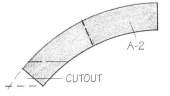
FIGURE 4: Curved Template A-2

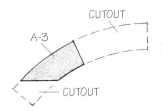
FIGURE 5: Curved Template A-3

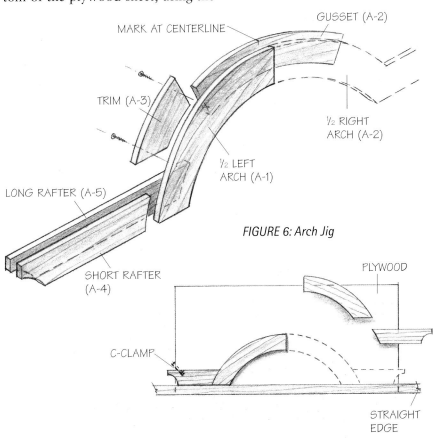
FIGURE 6: Arch Jig

The spectacular yellow Swamp Jessamine is native to the southeast United States. It flowers in the spring and again in the fall.

same technique shown in figure 3 in the Gateway Arbor project, page 76. After you've drawn the arch outlines, replace the straightedge at the bottom of the jig and secure it with a few screws or nails.

Testing the Fit of the Pieces

19. As figure 6 shows, each of the three arches is comprised of two side assemblies that are laminated together. To test the fit of all nine individual pieces for each arch, you can dry-assemble the parts in the plywood jig. Start by assembling all the pieces for one arch (A-1 through A-5) by placing the pieces for one side assembly on the outline you drew on the plywood jig in the previous step. Then arrange the pieces for the matching side assembly on top of the first assembly. The straightedge will help you align the pieces accurately. If there is any problem with the fit of the pieces at this stage, correct it now. Check the remaining arches in the same manner, positioning all the pieces in the jig for each arch and checking the fit of the joints.

20. Once assured that the pieces fit, place all the pieces for one arch on the jig and clamp the rafter pieces to prevent parts from shifting, as shown in figure 6. Drill two pilot holes for 1¼" screws through each of the top arch pieces and into the pieces underneath. You'll use these pilot holes to reposition the pieces accurately in the next step. To assemble the arches, you'll need approximately forty-six 1¼" deck screws per arch. The screws should be set flush with the sur-

face and arranged in a symmetrical pattern, as shown in figure 1.

Gluing the Arch Pieces

21. Leave the bottom pieces in place. Remove the top pieces and drive 1¼" screws partway through the pilot holes you made in the previous step. Leave approximately ¼" of the screw protruding from the bottom faces of the pieces. Spread glue on the adjoining faces of the top and bottom pieces. Reposition the top pieces by aligning the screws with the pilot holes on the bottom pieces. Then drive the screws through the top pieces and into the bottom pieces to secure them to each other.

22. Once you've driven all the screws in the first side, flip the arch over and drive screws for the opposite side. Work quickly and don't stop until you've finished assembling the whole arch. The screws will squeeze some of the glue out from the edges of the pieces. Wipe off any excess glue with a damp cloth as you tighten the screws. When all the screws are in, set the arch aside on a flat surface to dry. Place heavy objects on top of it to keep it flat. And make sure to wipe any excess glue off the plywood jig before starting on the next arch.

23. Repeat steps 19 through 22 for the other two arches. Remove the heavy objects on the first arch, then set the other two arches on top of the first arch and weigh down the stack with the heavy objects.

24. When the glue is dry, use a wood rasp and 100-grit sandpaper to smooth the sawn edges, but be careful not to round over the edges.

Cutting and Assembling the Decorative Chevrons

25. The mitered chevron pieces are 7" from long point to long point and you'll need to cut them precisely. Use a table saw or a miter saw with a stop to make the 45° angle cuts. You need 11 pairs of chevrons per pillar, for a total of 44 pairs for the four pillars.

26. For each pair, hold one piece in a bench vise while holding the other in position and drill two pilot holes for 2" screws across the mitered joint. Then add glue to the joint and drive two screws through the pilot holes to secure the assembly. Wipe off any excess glue.

Assembling the Posts and Chevrons

27. Each pair of posts (C) is assembled with 11 pairs of chevrons between the two posts, with the points of the chevrons facing up. Retrieve the plywood jig you used to assemble the arch pieces in step 18 and lay it down on a flat surface long enough to handle the posts. Place two of the posts side by side on the plywood. Put one post against the straightedge on the jig with its top edge flush with the edge of the plywood. Hold that post in place with C-clamps.

28. Place the top chevron between the posts, its pointed end aligned with the edge of the plywood and the end of the clamped post. Place another chevron between the posts several feet from the first one, to help keep the posts correctly

spaced apart. Now clamp the second post to the plywood.

29. Use the measurements in figure 1 and draw marks on both posts where the other chevrons will be attached. Measure the intervals carefully so the pieces will be spaced correctly.

30. To secure the chevrons to the posts, go back to the first chevron already in place, drill pilot holes and toenail two 2" screws through both legs of the chevron and into the side of the posts, as shown in figure 1. Screw the other chevrons into place, attaching them at the marks on the posts as you go. When you've finished attaching them, before you remove the post assembly from the jig, use the chevrons already in place to trace their positions on the plywood. You'll use these marks to install the chevrons for the next three post assemblies.

31. Repeat steps 27 through 30 for the other three post assemblies.

Setting the Post Assemblies

32. Call in your helpers. See Preparing the Site (page 23) and Digging Postholes (page 26), and refer to this project's figure 1 on page 86 for dimensions. Dig the holes for the posts.

33. Place the four post assemblies in the ground. Make sure they are all plumb and level with one another, and temporarily brace the posts in place with ground braces. Position the braces out of the way by placing them on the inside of the arbor, below where the arches will be, so that they won't interfere with your work in the next steps.

Cutting and Installing the Beams and Side Pieces

34. The beams (D) and side pieces (E) are the same length so it's efficient to cut them at the same time. Use the table saw or the miter saw with a stop to cut them to the dimensions indicated in the cutting list. Set the side pieces aside for now.

35. Two identical L-shaped jigs (shown in fig. 1) will help you hold the beams (D) in place while you attach them to the posts. Make the jigs from scrap 2 x 4 stock.

36. Call back your helpers. To attach the first beam, clamp the jigs at the top of each post to hold the beam in place, as shown in figure 1. Using the stepladder, raise the beam and place its ends in the notches of the jigs. Nudge the posts in against the ends of the beam to get a tight fit. Drill two pilot holes at the ends of the beam and toenail two 3" screws

Wide red ribbon and evergreens festoon a country arbor. Add mini-lights to welcome guests at night.

through the holes and into the posts.

37. Reposition the jigs to install the next beam, and repeat step 36 for all the beams.

Attaching the Side Pieces

38. Like the beams, the side pieces (E) fit between the post assemblies, as shown in figure 1. They also are aligned at the same angle as the legs of the chevrons. To support the ends of the side pieces at the correct angle as you attach them to the posts, use two pieces of 12" long scrap 2 x 4 as support blocks. Align the blocks with the legs of the chevrons and clamp the blocks in place, as shown in figure 1. Position the side pieces on top of the support blocks. Start with the chevron just above the chevron closest to the ground. Move and align the support blocks with the chevrons as you go. Drill pilot holes and toenail the ends of the side pieces to the posts with 3" screws.

39. Go around the posts and backfill to secure the structure. Remove the temporary bracing.

Cutting and Attaching the Roof Pieces

40. Cut the roof pieces (F) according to the cutting list. Starting from the center of the arches, attach the roof pieces to each arch with 2" screws, spacing the roof pieces every 3", as shown in figure 1. All the roof pieces overhang the front and back by 5". The last roof pieces should overhang the ends of the arches slightly on both sides. When you've finished, have a party to celebrate your magnificent accomplishment!

Roses! Roses! Roses!

Many people think the only reason to build an arbor is to have a place to show off their roses! Love for roses, with their incredible beauty and fragrance, seems ingrained in the human spirit. Roses are one of the oldest plants on earth. Fossilized remains show it to be at least 35 million years old. It's also the flower that's been cultivated the longest, perhaps beginning some 5,000 years ago in China's gardens. All throughout its long history the rose has been given a place of honor. The Egyptians offered it to

White Banksian Rose

Isis, the goddess who taught them the wonders of medicine. Legend says when a drop of sweat from the prophet Mohammed fell on the ground, it became a rose. Benedictine monks nurtured the rose in their monasteries, making it a symbol of their devotion. Ancient Persians were the first to extract rose oil; many centuries later, the French re-discovered the secret and created the world-famous perfume industry.

Although roses grow wild over most of the Northern hemisphere, the popular roses in today's gardens have two roots: Europe/Middle East and China. The "western" roses, although beautiful, bloomed only once a year. Then in 1792 a new rose was introduced into Europe from China—it was astonishing because it continued to bloom all summer long.

Rosette Delizy

Roses don't climb naturally: they need supports such as arbors and trellises to help them grow vertically. They have long pliable canes that can be tied to train their growth pattern. When they're tied horizontally they actually produce more flowers, which is why you often see an abundance of roses on the top of an arbor.

There are three categories of climbing roses: ramblers, trailing roses, and true climbers. Ramblers are quite vigorous, meaning they can be heavy on a structure, and generally have smaller blooms. Trailing roses are quite hardy, with medium size blooms, about 2 to 3 inches across. True climbers, as they're called, have large flowers, a few in each cluster. Some climbers bloom for just a few weeks each season. Others, called pillar roses, bloom all season long.

Roses can grow in regions that have cold winters, but they must have at least six hours a day of sunshine during their growing period. Water them in the early morning; this helps prevent sunburning the leaves during the heat of the day, and reduces moisture at night that can cause blackspot and mildew. Some roses are finicky and demanding. Others are hardy and survive relatively well in a state of benign neglect. There are roses to suit anyone's gardening skill, and an astonishing selection of colors, size, and fragrance; there are even some thornless varieties. If you've been dreaming of a rose arbor, maybe now's the time to start building one yourself in your own garden.

Dream Weaver

STATELY ARBOR

Adapted Design by Olivier Rollin

This elegant plantation-style arbor looks right at home in traditional well-kept gardens, especially in green areas large enough to match its stately size. We simplified the design of the molding and increased the arbor's sturdiness by adding braces at the top.

Note: The postholes for this project are 36" deep to account for the extra girth and mass of the arbor, as shown in figure 1. Also, we specified stock chair rail molding for dressing up the posts, but practically any available molding will do as long as its dimensions are similar.

WHAT YOU NEED

Basic Tool Kit
Digging Kit
Additional Tools
- $3/32$" drill bit for piloting $2\frac{1}{2}$" deck screws
- $1/8$" drill bit for piloting $3\frac{1}{2}$" deck screws
- $1/4$" drill bit, at least 5" in length, for piloting the $3/8$" lag screws
- 1" spade bit
- Jigsaw
- Circular saw
- Miter saw
- Table saw

Material and Supplies
- Water-resistant wood glue
- 1 piece posterboard, 28 x 44"
- Post ground braces

Hardware
- $1/2$ lb. galvanized 6d finish nails
- A few spare 16d common nails
- 1 lb. of $2\frac{1}{2}$" decks screws
- 1 lb. $3\frac{1}{2}$" deck screws
- 4 $3/8$" lag screws, 6" long, and washers

CUTTING LIST

Code	Description	Qty.	Dimensions	Cut from
A	Posts	4	$5\frac{1}{2}$" x $5\frac{1}{2}$" x 132"	2 pcs. 6 x 6 x 12'
B	Crossbeams	4	$1\frac{1}{2}$" x $7\frac{1}{4}$" x 118"	4 pcs. 2 x 8 x 10'
C	Braces	4	$5\frac{1}{2}$" x $5\frac{1}{2}$" x 34"	2 pcs. 6 x 6 x 8'
D	Roof Pieces	7	$1\frac{1}{2}$" x $7\frac{1}{4}$" x 80"	7 pcs. 2 x 8 x 8'
E	Baseboards	16	$1\frac{1}{2}$" x $5\frac{1}{2}$" x $8\frac{1}{2}$"	2 pcs. 2 x 6 x 8'
F	Molding	80	$3/4$" x $1\frac{1}{4}$" x 8"	60' of ready-made chair rail molding
G	Finials	4	6" diameter x 8" long	Ready made, with lag screw

INSTRUCTIONS
Cutting the Pieces

1. Cut all the pieces to the dimensions in the cutting list, including those with scrolled cuts such as the crossbeams (B) and the roof pieces (D). The braces (C) have 45° miter cuts at both ends and are 34" long from the long point to the long point of the miters. Leave the molding (F) for now; you'll cut and install it later.

2. You'll need to make a template to help with laying out the curved cuts on the crossbeams (B) and the roof pieces (D). Enlarge the template shown in figure

FIGURE 1:
Stately Arbor

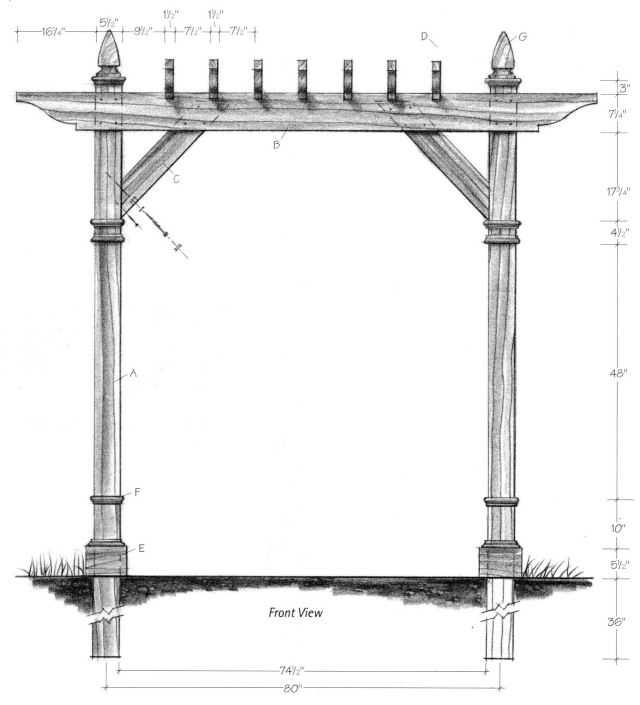

Front View

2 to full size on the posterboard, then cut out the template with scissors or a sharp knife. Use the same template to trace the profile on the crossbeams and the roof pieces onto the stock. Cut out the profiles with the jigsaw.

3. Lay out the dadoes on the roof pieces (D) as shown in figure 1, but don't cut them at this point.

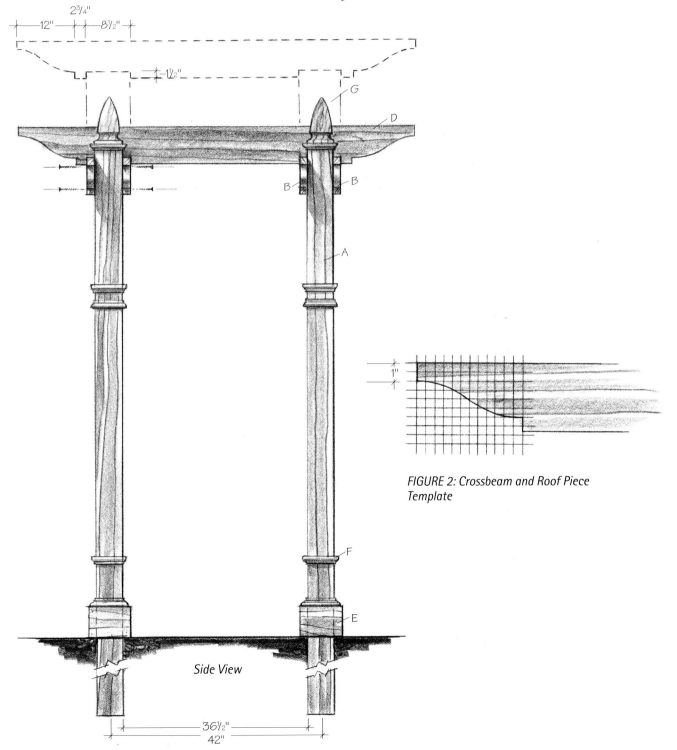

FIGURE 2: *Crossbeam and Roof Piece Template*

Side View

The Rouge Cardinal Clematis has gorgeous velvety crimson flowers that bloom in late summer.

Positioning the Posts (A) and Installing Temporary Bracing

4. Call in your helpers. See Preparing the Site (page 23) and Digging Postholes (page 26) and refer to figure 1 for dimensions. Dig the holes for the posts. Once the holes are dug, position the posts (A) in the holes, making sure they're level with each other. Brace the posts securely with the temporary ground post braces.

Attaching the Crossbeams

5. Once the posts are in the ground, attach the crossbeams (B). Measure and mark 10¼" from the top of each post.

6. In this step you'll install the crossbeams. Call in your helpers to assist. Make sure during the process that all four beams are level and aligned with each other. On the crossbeams, make a mark 16¼" from both ends. Starting at the two front posts, drive a 16d nail

halfway into the front of each post on the 10¼" marks you made in step 5. Position one crossbeam on top of the nails and against the posts, and adjust the beam so that the 16¼" marks on the beam align with the outside of the posts. Adjust the spacing of the posts if necessary to fit the marks. Have your helpers hold the crossbeam in place as you drill pilot holes and drive 3½" screws through the crossbeam into each post. Repeat for the other three crossbeams. Pull out the supporting 16d nails.

Attaching the Braces

7. You'll attach one brace (C) to one arch at a time. See figure 1 and note that the upper part of the brace fits between the crossbeams (B), and the lower mitered end butts into the side of the post (A). Start by using the spade bit to countersink a 1" deep hole into the

An elegant, unified look is created in a garden when the structures are similar in style. This gateway arch is smaller in scale, but follows similar principles in design, as the Stately Arbor. The theme is carried out in the fence, with its posts topped by finials.

mitered area of the brace, centered on the face of the brace and 4" from the tip of its miter. (See fig. 1.) Drill a $\frac{1}{4}$" pilot hole in the center of the countersink and through the brace. Repeat this drilling procedure for the other three braces.

8. Make a mark on the posts $17\frac{3}{4}$" from the bottom edge of the crossbeams. Insert one of the braces between the crossbeams and adjust it so its lower miter butts against the post and is level with your mark. Drill pilot holes and drive two $2\frac{1}{2}$" screws $1\frac{1}{2}$" from the bottom of the brace and into the post, then drill a pilot hole and drive a single $2\frac{1}{2}$" screw through the crossbeam and into the upper portion of the brace to temporarily hold it in place. Check that the miter fits snugly against the post.

9. Finish securing the bottom of the brace to the post with the lag screw. Using the countersunk hole as a guide, drill a $\frac{1}{4}$" pilot hole into the post and drive a 6" lag screw through the brace and into the post. The head of the lag should sit below the surface of the brace in its countersunk hole.

10. Attach the upper part of the brace to the crossbeams by drilling pilot holes and driving $3\frac{1}{2}$" screws through the beam and into the brace, as shown in figure 1. Make sure to drive screws through both sides of the crossbeams.

11. Repeat steps 8 through 10 to install the remaining three braces.

Attaching the Roof Pieces

12. Each roof piece (D) extends $16\frac{1}{4}$" beyond the posts, and each straddles a pair of crossbeams, as shown in figure 1. Start by positioning the roof pieces onto the crossbeams and check that their dado layouts you drew in step 3 line up with beams. Cut the dadoes, fit them over the crossbeams, and adjust if necessary. (Refer to the instructions on making dado cuts on page 19.) Drill pilot holes and secure the roof pieces with $2\frac{1}{2}$" screws driven at an angle through the roof pieces and into the crossbeams.

Adding the Baseboards and Molding

13. Refer to the dimensions in figure 1 to cut and miter the baseboards (E). Use the table saw to cut the miters, aiming for cuts that are a pencil line's thickness longer than needed, to avoid gaps at the mitered corners. Drill pilot holes and secure the baseboard pieces level with the ground at the bottom of the posts using $2\frac{1}{2}$" screws.

14. Using a stepladder prepare to attach the molding (F) around the posts. Refer to figure 1 to mark the posts for the height of each series of molding. Use the miter saw to cut the miters. Attach the molding by drilling pilot holes and driving 6d nails through the molding into the posts. Set the nail heads with a nailset.

Adding the Finials

15. Add the four finials (G) at the tops of the posts to set off the design. Using a stepladder, drill pilot holes for the finials' lag bolts into the ends of the posts and install the finials into the holes. Finally, climb down to admire your work. Enjoy an ice-cold mint julep and be languorous.

QUIET TIME BENCH ARBOR

Adapted Design by Olivier Rollin

Is it a display shelf, a bench, a trellis, or an arbor? Yes, and more— a perfect place to sit by yourself and relax after a busy day. The gently curved parts give the project its distinctive look.

WHAT YOU NEED

Basic Tool Kit
Additional Tools
- $^3/_{32}$" drill bit for piloting $2^1/_2$" deck screws
- $^1/_8$" drill bit for piloting 3" deck screws
- Jigsaw
- Circular saw
- Shovel

Materials and Supplies
- 1 piece of scrap, $^3/_4$" thick
- 1 piece posterboard, 28" x 44"

Hardware
- 2 lb. $2^1/_2$" deck screws
- 2 lb. 3" deck screws

CUTTING LIST

Code	Description	Qty.	Dimensions	Cut from
A	Bases	4	$1^1/_2$" x $5^1/_2$" x 48"	2 pcs. 2 x 6 x 8'
B	Posts	8	$1^1/_2$" x $3^1/_2$" x 87"	4 pcs. 2 x 4 x 8'
C	Lattice Pieces	20	$1^1/_2$" x $1^1/_2$" x $23^1/_2$"	10 pcs. 2 x 2 x 4'
D	Arches	2	$1^1/_2$" x $7^1/_4$" x 77"	2 pcs. 2 x 8 x 8'
E	Bench Supports	2	$1^1/_2$" x $3^1/_2$" x 30"	1 pc. 2 x 4 x 4'
F	Bench Slats			
F-1	Short Slats	2	$1^1/_2$" x $3^1/_2$" x 46"	2 pcs. 2 x 4 x 8'
F-2	Long Slats	7	$1^1/_2$" x $3^1/_2$" x 55"	4 pcs. 2 x 4 x 10'
G	Braces	4	$1^1/_2$" x $5^1/_2$" x 12"	1 pc. 2 x 6 x 8'
I	Roof Pieces	7	$1^1/_2$" x $3^1/_2$" x 40"	4 pcs. 2 x 4 x 8'
H	Center Support	1	$1^1/_2$" x $3^1/_2$" x 28"	1 pc. 2 x 4 x 8'

INSTRUCTIONS
Cutting the Pieces

1. Refer to the cutting list to cut all the parts except for the roof pieces (I), which will be cut and adjusted later. The templates shown in figure 2 need to be enlarged to size (see the section on enlarging templates on page 18). Cut out the templates and trace around them on the lumber for the arches (D), braces (G), and the roof pieces (H). Use the jigsaw to cut out the arch pieces and the braces, following the layout lines. You can cut the roof pieces to length according to the cutting list, but don't cut the scrolled area at this point. Note that the two bench supports (E) have 30° angled cuts at both ends, as shown in figure 1.

Making the Bases

2. There are two bases, each comprised of two 48" long pieces of 2 x 6 lumber.

FIGURE 1:
Quiet Time Bench Arbor

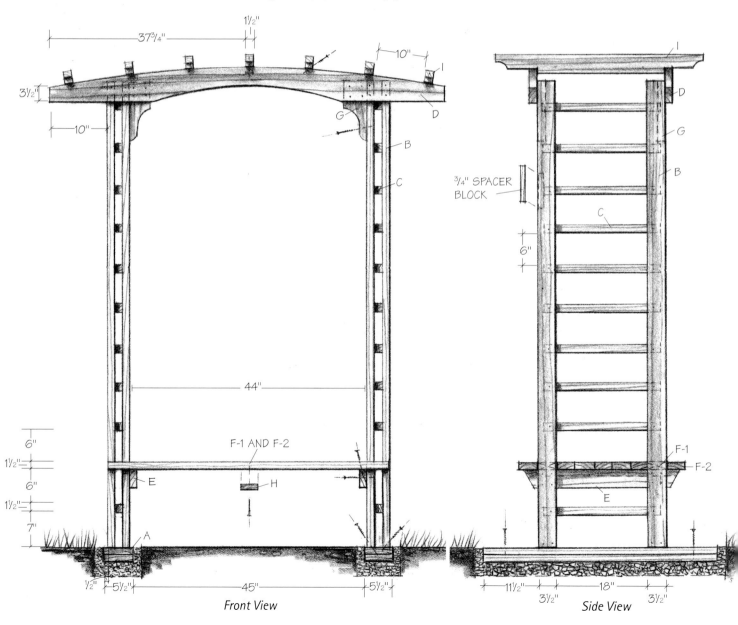

Front View

Side View

Assemble the pieces with 2½" screws. Refer to figure 1 for dimensions and dig two shallow trenches 7" deep, 12" wide, and 60" long. Shovel 4" of gravel into the trenches, making sure the gravel is level. Position both bases in the trenches so they are level, parallel to each other, and 45" apart. Adjust the gravel underneath if necessary.

Making the Arbor Sides

3. The sides of the arbor are composed of the posts (B) and lattice pieces (C). Build one side at a time. Take two of the 2 x 4 posts and use the dimensions in figure 1 to mark both posts where the lattice pieces (C) will be attached, starting 7" up from the bottom of the post. Notice there is no lattice piece where the bench slats will go through the posts.

4. Lay the two posts on the ground side by side, 18" apart, with the marked sides up. Position the lattice pieces on the marks on the posts. Drill pilot holes on each piece 2" from both of its ends. Drive 2½" screws through the lattice pieces to attach them to the posts. To keep all the ends of the lattice pieces precisely ¾" from the edges of the posts, use a ¾" thick piece of scrap to help space them as you screw them fast, as shown in figure 1.

5. Once all the lattice pieces are attached to a pair of posts, position the second pair of posts atop the lattice pieces and aligned with the first posts, sandwiching the lattice pieces between them. Drill pilot holes through the second set of posts and the lattice pieces

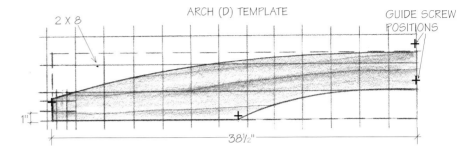

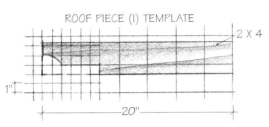

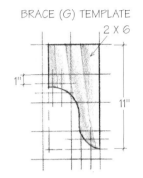

FIGURE 2: Arbor Templates

below. Place the holes at the center of the posts to avoid hitting the screws already in place. Then attach the top posts to the lattice pieces with 3" screws.

6. On the two posts now facing up, measure and make a mark at 14½" from their bottom ends.

7. Center and attach one bench support (E) on your marks, drilling pilot holes and securing the supports to the posts with 3" screws, as shown in figure 1.

8. Repeat steps 4 through 7 to make the second arbor side.

Attaching the Short Bench Slats

9. Call in your helpers. On the ground, prop up the two sides parallel to each other. Take one short slat (F-1) and position it between the sides and on top of the bench supports (E). Center the slat with the inside of the posts and secure it temporarily to the bench supports with C-clamps. Make sure that both ends of

The Freda Anemone Clematis is ideal for bench arbors. It provides a wonderful summer color and a sweet fragrance.

the slat fit snugly against the posts. Drill pilot holes at both ends and drive 3" screws through the slat and into the bench supports. Repeat for the other short bench slat. Leave the remaining bench slats off for now; you want to keep the structure as lightweight as possible for the next few steps.

Attaching the Arches and Braces

10. On one arch, make a mark 10" from each end. Use the marks to position the arch such that it extends 10" past the sides, with its bottom edge 3½" down from the top of the sides. (See fig. 1.) Hold the arch in place temporarily with C-clamps. Check that the arch and posts are perpendicular to each other using a carpenter's square. Drill pilot holes through the arch and drive 3" screws through the holes and into the edges of the posts of the sides. Use two screws per post, as shown in figure 1.

11. With the arch-and-post assembly still on the ground, you can install one of the braces (G). The braces are attached to the inner posts of the sides and to the backs of the arches. Hold two of the braces in place temporarily with C-clamps to the back of one arch, against the inside posts.

12. Drill pilot holes through the back of the braces to attach them to the back of the arch with 3" screws. Then drill a single pilot hole through the edge of each brace and drive 3" screws through the brace and into the post.

13. Turn over the structure, and repeat steps 10 through 12 to attach the second arch and the remaining pair of braces.

Installing the Arbor

14. Call in your helper. Stand the arbor upright and center it on the two bases. Secure the arbor to the bases by drilling angled pilot holes through the posts and toenailing 3" screws through the holes and into the bases.

Completing the Arbor Bench

15. To complete the bench, attach the remaining long slat pieces (F-2) to the bench supports (E), drilling pilot holes and using 3" screws. To stiffen the slats, attach the center support (H) by temporarily securing it with C-clamps to the underside of the bench. Then drill pilot holes and drive 2½" screws through the support and into each slat.

Attaching the Roof Pieces

16. Refer to the measurements in figure 1 to mark the positions of the roof pieces (I) at the tops of the arches. For clarity on the figure, we drew only the middle roof piece so you could see how it is positioned in relation to the arches. The bottoms of the roof pieces are cut to fit between the backs of the arches. Check the template lines you drew in step 1 on the roof pieces by placing each piece on top of the arch where it will go. Adjust the lines if necessary before cutting out the scrolled area with the jigsaw.

17. Replace the roof pieces on top of the arches, drill angled pilot holes, and toenail 2½" screws through the roof pieces and into the arches. Kick off your shoes, sit down, and enjoy the rare luxury of being alone after a job well done.

WOOD AND WIRE BENCH ARBOR

Design by Jane Wilson

Wire fencing

adds an airy touch to this easy-to-make bench arbor. Throw fabric over the wire arch for instant shade. Plant morning glories or other quick-growers to enjoy shade by season's end.

The fast-growing Blue Dawn Morning Glory has a remarkably long blooming season, from summer all the way to frost.

WHAT YOU NEED

Basic Tool Box
Digging Kit
Additional Tools
- $\frac{3}{32}$" drill bit for piloting 2" screws
- $\frac{1}{4}$" drill bit
- Miter box or miter saw (optional)

Materials and Supplies
- Roll of 24"-wide vinyl-coated wire fencing, with 2" x 3" mesh openings

Hardware
- 8 10d finish nails
- $\frac{1}{2}$ lb. 2" deck screws
- 4 carriage bolts, $\frac{1}{4}$" x $4\frac{1}{2}$" long, with matching nuts and washers

CUTTING LIST

Code	Description	Qty.	Dimensions	Cut from
A	Uprights	4	$1\frac{1}{2}$" x $1\frac{1}{2}$" x 60"	4 pcs. 2 x 2 x 8'
B	Upright Supports	4	$\frac{3}{4}$" x $1\frac{1}{2}$" x 60"	4 pcs. 1 x 2 x 8'
C	Arch Crosspieces	6	$1\frac{1}{2}$" x $1\frac{1}{2}$" x 24"	3 pcs. 2 x 2 x 8'
D	Crosspiece Supports	6	$\frac{3}{4}$" x $1\frac{1}{2}$" x 24"	1pc. 1 x 2 x 2'
E	Bench Cleats	2	$1\frac{1}{2}$" x $3\frac{1}{2}$" x 24"	1 pc. 2 x 4 x 8'
F	Bench Slats	6	$\frac{3}{4}$" x $3\frac{1}{2}$" x 48"	3 pc. 1 x 4 x 8'
G	Bench Braces	4	$1\frac{1}{2}$" x $1\frac{1}{2}$" x 12"	2 x 2' waste

INSTRUCTIONS

Preparing the Site and Cutting the Parts

1. Clear the site and rake it free of debris. (See Preparing the Site on page 23.)

2. Cut all the pieces according to the cutting list. Cut the longest parts first, then use the leftover 2 x 2 stock to cut the mitered bench braces (G) shown in figure 1. Use the miter box to cut 45° miters on both ends of the braces, checking that each brace measures 12" from the long point to long point of the miters.

3. Wearing protective gloves, use the wire cutters to cut a 16' length of wire fencing from the roll.

Assembling the Sides and the Wire Arch

4. Lay out the 16' length of wire fencing in the center of your leveled site area. Starting at one end of the wire, sandwich the long edges of the wire between a pair of uprights (A) and a pair of upright supports (B), making sure the edges of the wire are flush with the outer edges of the uprights. Position the uprights under the wire and the upright supports on top. Use the combination square to check that the ends of all the uprights are even. The drill pilot holes every 8" or so and drive 2" screws through the supports and into the uprights, taking care to avoid the wire. Repeat at the opposite end of the wire to install the remaining two uprights and corresponding upright supports.

5. With the assembly still on the ground and the upright supports (B) on top, attach the arch crosspieces (C) and the crosspiece supports (D). Working at one end of the assembly, position a crosspiece support (D) across the top ends of the two upright supports (B), with its ends even with the outside edges of the supports. Slip an arch crosspiece (D) underneath, aligning it with the crosspiece support above it and with the wire fencing in between. Drill pilot holes through the crosspiece support and drive a 2" screw into the arch crosspiece at each end and one in the center. Repeat at the other end of the assembly.

6. On each end of the assembly, measure 7" from first set of crosspieces and repeat the sandwich assembly of arch crosspieces (C) and crosspiece supports (D). Then measure another 7" from those assemblies and install the remaining two crosspiece assemblies. You should now have six crosspiece assemblies installed at equal intervals along the fencing, as shown in figure 1.

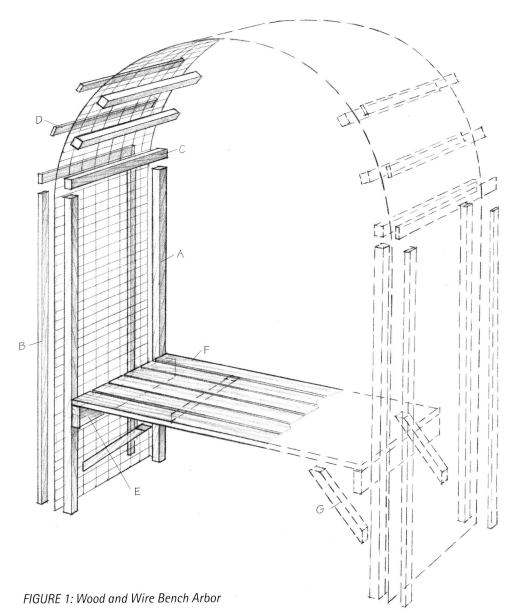

FIGURE 1: Wood and Wire Bench Arbor

Attaching the Bench Cleats

7. Carefully turn the assembly over so the uprights (A) and arch crosspieces (C) are on top. Measure and mark 16" up from the ends of the uprights and place the top edges of each bench cleat (E) on your marks. The ends of the bench cleats should be even with the outside edges of

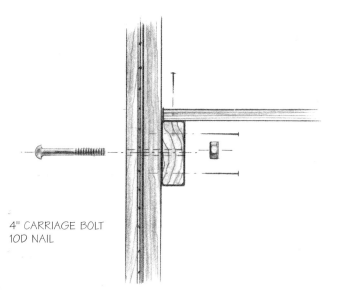

4" CARRIAGE BOLT
10D NAIL

FIGURE 2: Attaching the Bench Cleat and Bench Slats

the uprights. Use C-clamps to temporarily secure the ends of the cleats to the uprights.

8. Secure the bench cleats to the uprights with a 4" carriage bolt through the ends of each cleat, as shown in figure 2. (E). To install each bolt, drill a ¼" hole through the cleat and the upright, centering the hole on the upright. Slip the carriage bolt through the hole so its nut end will be inside the arch, and tighten with the wrench. (See fig. 2.) To further stabilize the connection, hammer in a pair of 10d nails through the cleat and into the upright. Remove the clamps, then repeat the clamping and drilling procedure to secure the second bench cleat at the opposite end of the arbor assembly.

Erecting the Arbor and Attaching the Bench Slats

9. Call in your helpers. Turn the arbor assembly over, and carefully stand it upright so the sides of the arbor are roughly 4'

Wood and wire combine to make a structure that is both solid and airy.

apart and the wire arch bends upward in a graceful curve. Position one of the bench slats (F) between the two sides and on top of the bench cleats, with the ends of the slat tight against two opposing uprights. Check that the outside edge of the slat is even with the outside edge of the uprights. With this first slat in position, drill pilot holes and drive a pair of 2" screws through each end of the slat and into the bench cleats below. Install a second slat on the opposite side of the arbor, aligning it as you did the first slat, so it's tight against the uprights and flush with their outside edges. Finish installing the remaining four bench slats by laying them on top of the bench cleats and arranging them so the spacing between them and the two outer slats is equal, then drill pilot holes and secure them with 2" screws.

Attaching the Bench Braces

10. To strengthen the structure and complete the arbor, install the four bench braces (G) underneath the seat slats, as shown in figure 1. Before installing the braces, use the carpenter's square to check that the bench surface is square to the sides of the arbor. Then hold each brace so its mitered ends are tight against an upright and the underside of an outer bench slat, drill angled pilot holes through the miters, and toenail a 2" screw through each miter and into the upright and the bench slat. Have a seat—you're done!

CONVERSATION ARBOR

Adapted Design by Olivier Rollin

With its sheltering stay-a-while sides and face-to-face benches, this arbor was designed to cultivate the fine art of conversation. We changed a few details to simplify the construction, so you could spend less time working and more time talking.

The Summer Snow Mandevilla blooms all summer.

WHAT YOU NEED

Basic Tool Kit

Digging Tool Kit

Additional Tools
- $^3/_{32}$" drill bit for piloting 2" and $2^1/_2$" deck screws
- $^1/_8$" drill pit for piloting 3" screws
- Jigsaw
- Circular saw

Materials and Supplies
- 1 piece posterboard, 28" x 44"
- 1 piece scrap 2 x 4 x 8'

Hardware
- 1 lb. 2" deck screws
- 2 lbs. $2^1/_2$" deck screws
- 1 lb. 3" deck screws

CUTTING LIST

Code	Description	Qty.	Dimensions	Cut from
A	Posts	8	$3^1/_2$" x $3^1/_2$" x $42^1/_2$"	1pc. 4 x 4 x 8'
A-1	Post Rails	4	$1^1/_2$" x $3^1/_2$" x 11"	1 pcs. 2 x 4 x 4'
B	Seat Frames	2		B-1and B-2 from:
B-1	Long Pieces	4	$1^1/_2$" x $3^1/_2$" x $46^1/_2$"	3 pcs. 2 x 4 x 8'
B-2	Short Pieces	6	$1^1/_2$" x $3^1/_2$" x 11"	
B-3	Seatboards	6	$^3/_4$" x $5^1/_2$" x $46^1/_2$"	3 pcs. 1 x 6 x 8'
C	Backrests	2		
C-1	Stiles	4	$1^1/_2$" x $3^1/_2$" x 64"	C-1, C-2, C-3, C-4, & C-5 from: 2 x 4 x 10'
C-2	Top Rails	2	$1^1/_2$" x $3^1/_2$" x $39^1/_2$"	
C-3	Mid and Lower Rails	8	$1^1/_2$" x $3^1/_2$" x $14^1/_2$"	
C-4	Support Rails	6	$1^1/_2$" x $3^1/_2$" x $46^1/_2$"	
C-5	Center Stiles	2	$1^1/_2$" x $3^1/_2$" x $26^1/_2$"	
C-6	Backboards	8	$^3/_4$" x $5^1/_2$" x $46^1/_2$"	C6 and C-7 from: 5 pcs. 1 x 6 x 8'
C-7	Scrolled Backboards	2	$^3/_4$" x $5^1/_2$" x $46^1/_2$"	
D	Side Walls	4		
D-1	Scrolled Wallboards	4	$^3/_4$" x $11^1/_4$" x $29^3/_4$"	1 pc. 1 x 12 x 10'
D-2	Middle Wallboards	4	$^3/_4$" x $7^1/_4$" x $83^1/_2$"	4 pcs. 1 x 8 x 8'
D-3	Outside Wallboards	2	$^3/_4$" x $5^1/_2$" x $83^1/_2$"	4 pcs. 1 x 6 x 8'
D-4	Cleats	2	$1^1/_2$" x $3^1/_2$" x $7^1/_2$"	1 pc. 2 x 4 x 4'
E	Arches	4	$1^1/_2$" x $11^1/_4$" x $95^1/_2$"	1 pc. 2 x 12 x 8'
F	Roof Pieces	8	$1^1/_2$" x $3^1/_2$" x 59"	4 pcs. 1 x 4 x 10'

INSTRUCTIONS

Cutting the Pieces

1. Cut all the pieces to match the cutting list. You will need to make templates for the scrolled pieces (C-7, D-1) and the arches (E). Enlarge the templates in figure 2 onto the posterboard and cut them out. (See the instructions for enlarging templates on page 18.) Once you've made the posterboard templates, use them to lay out the scrolled parts on the stock, then cut along your layout lines with the jigsaw.

Digging the Holes and Installing the Posts

2. Refer to Preparing the Site (page 23) and Digging Postholes (page 26) and project figure 1 on page 112. Call in your helper. Dig the holes for the eight posts (A). Set the posts into the holes and check that the tops of the posts are 12½" above ground. Make sure the posts are level and plumb and all the tops are aligned and even with each other. Backfill around the posts and lightly tamp down the dirt, just enough to hold the posts in position.

3. Attach the post rails (A-1) flush with the outsides of the posts and 11½" from the tops of the posts, as shown in figure 3. To secure the rails, drill angled pilot holes through their ends and toenail 2½" screws through the holes and into the posts.

Making and Installing the Seat Frames

4. Assemble the two seat frames (B) next, as shown in figures 1 and 3. Align the five parts of each frame (B-1 and B-2), drill pilot holes through the joints, and drive 3" screws through the joints to secure them. Attach the frames to the tops of the posts with 3" screws, toenailing them through the frames at an angle and into the posts. At this point, check that all the posts and frames are perpendicular to each other and plumb, then complete the backfilling by tamping down firmly so the posts are secured.

Building and Installing the Backrest Frames

5. Refer to figures 1 and 3 to see how all the pieces of the backrest (C) fit together. Make one frame at a time. Arrange the three support rails (C-4) on a flat surface, spacing them apart as shown in figure 3. Then position all of the frame parts (C-1 through C-5) on top of the support rails. Make sure that all the parts are snug and square with each other, and that the bottom support rail (C-4) extends 1½" past the bottom of the frame. This extension will help you in the next step when attaching the backrest frame to the seat frame. Assemble the frame by drilling pilot holes and driving 2½" screws through the top pieces and into the support rails. Repeat this procedure to build the second frame.

6. Position one completed backrest frame above a seat frame, as shown in figure 3. Make sure the frame is centered, then drill pilot holes and drive 3" screws through the extension of the bottom support rail (C-4) and into the back of the bench frame. To brace the backrest, temporarily screw two 2 x 4s, each

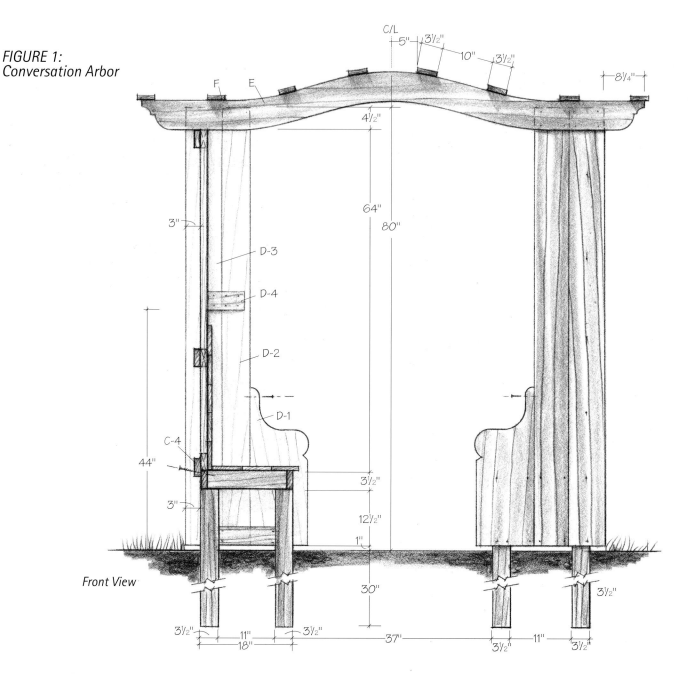

FIGURE 1:
Conversation Arbor

C/L

5" 3½" 10" 3½" 8¼"

F E

4½"

64"
80"

3"

D-3

D-4

D-2

D-1

C-4

44"

3½"

3"

12½"

1"

Front View

30"

3½"

3½" 11" 3½" 37" 11" 3½"
18" 3½" 3½"

about 2′ long, between the backrest frame and the seat frame. Attach the braces on the inside of the frames so they won't interfere with the next step. Repeat for the second backrest frame.

Installing the Side Walls

7. Starting with one side wall (D), first attach the outside wallboard (D-3). (See figs. 1 and 3.) Temporarily hold the wallboard in place with C-clamps, making sure it extends 3″ from the side of the post and is aligned with the bottom of the post rail (A-1). The top of the wallboard should extend 4½″ above the backrest frame, as shown in figure 1. Attach the wallboard by drilling pilot holes and driving 2½″ screws through

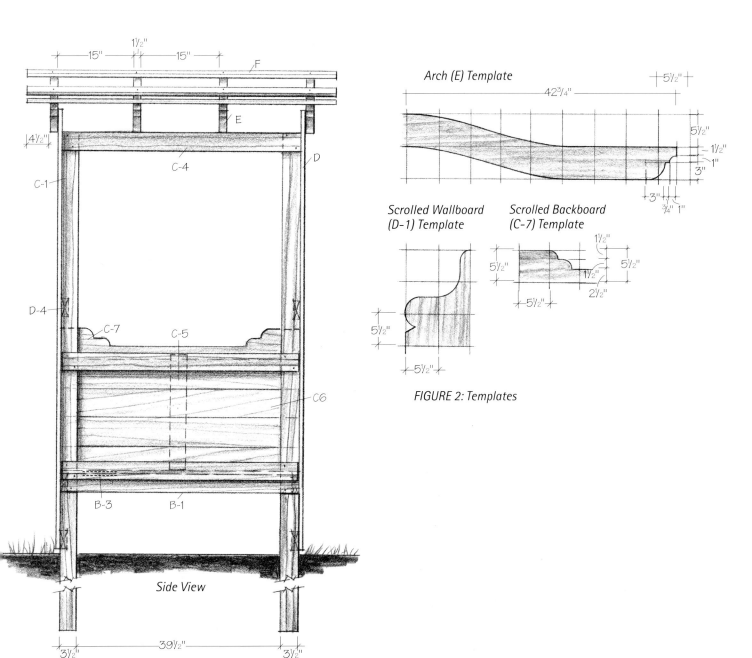

Arch (E) Template

42¾"

5½"

5½"

1½"

1"

3"

3"

¾" 1"

Scrolled Wallboard
(D-1) Template

Scrolled Backboard
(C-7) Template

5½"

1½"

5½"

1½"

2½"

5½"

5½"

5½"

FIGURE 2: Templates

15"

1½"

15"

F

E

4½"

C-4

C-1

D

D-4

C-7

C-5

C6

B-3

B-1

Side View

39½"

3½"

3½"

the wallboard and into the post, post rail, seat frame, and backrest frame.

8. Position the remaining wallboards (D-1 and D-2) so their bottom edges are even with the outside wallboard (D-3) you just installed. Secure these wallboards as before, drilling pilot holes and using 2½" screws to attach the parts to the post, post rail, and seat frame. To secure the top of the scrolled wallboard (D-1), drill a pilot hole through its upper edge and drive a 3" screw through it and into the edge of the middle wallboard (D-2). Refer to figure 1.

9. Attach a cleat (D-4) to the inside of the wall, locating it 44" above the ground, as shown in figures 1 and 3. Drill

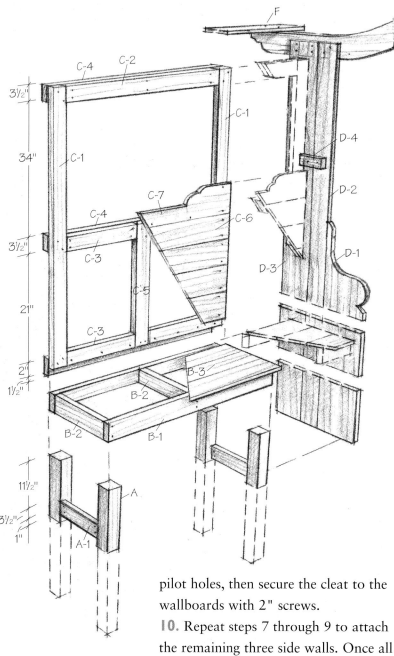

Dimension labels on figure:
3½"
34"
C-4 C-2
C-1
C-1
C-4
C-7
C-3
C-6
3½"
C-3
C-5
21"
C-3
2"
1½"
B-3
B-2
B-2
B-1
11½"
A
3½"
1"
A-1
F
E
D-4
D-2
D-1
D-3

FIGURE 3: Arbor Assembly

pilot holes, then secure the cleat to the wallboards with 2" screws.

10. Repeat steps 7 through 9 to attach the remaining three side walls. Once all the walls are in place, you can remove the bracing you installed in step 6.

Installing the Arches

11. Get your helper and the stepladder to help you with the arch installation. Refer to figures 1 and 3. Begin by installing one of the outside arches (E). Center the arch

and attach it to the outside of both side walls such that the top of the arch extends 1" above the top of the side walls. Use C-clamps to help hold the arch in position while you drill pilot holes and drive 2" screws from the inside of the side walls and into the arch. Repeat for the second outside arch. Once the outer arches are in place, measure from them and center the two middle arches on top of the backrest frames. Secure the middle arches by drilling angled pilot holes and toenailing 3" screws through the arches and into the frames.

Attaching the Roof Pieces

12. See figures 1 and 3 for the layout and position of the roof pieces (F). Drill pilot holes and attach the roof pieces to the arches with 2½" screws.

Installing the Bench Boards

13. Referring to figures 1 and 3, lay out and install the seatboards and backboards (B-3, C-6 and C-7) on both sides of the arbor. Start by installing the backboards, attaching each lower board first and working your way up. Drill pilot holes and secure the backboards to the backrest frame with 2" screws. Now reward yourself with a nice conversation with your helper. Should you add trays to hold cold drinks, or cushions for more comfort? And what kinds of plants should you decorate the arbor with? Beautiful purple morning glories to celebrate the sun? Or night-blooming jasmine for a scent of romance after sunset?

DOWN HOME POLE TRELLIS

Adapted Design by Olivier Rollin

This rustic trellis is perfect for helping vegetables and flowers grow up. A grouping of trellises gives the garden a lush, abundant look. They're so easy to make—go ahead and make a bundle.

FIGURE 1: Down Home Pole Trellis

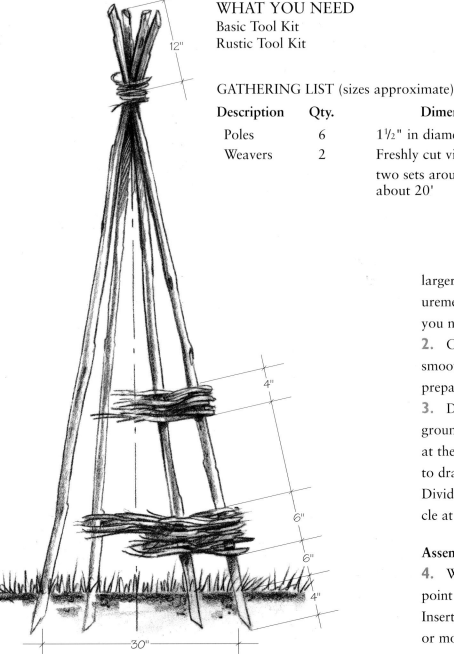

WHAT YOU NEED
Basic Tool Kit
Rustic Tool Kit

GATHERING LIST (sizes approximate)

Description	Qty.	Dimensions	Material
Poles	6	1½" in diameter and 78" long	Green or Dried
Weavers	2	Freshly cut vines, enough to lace two sets around the poles, about 20'	Green

larger trellis, you can modify the measurements and the amount of materials you need.

2. Clear the site of debris and make it smooth. Refer to the information on preparing the site, page 23.

3. Draw a 30" diameter circle on the ground. Use the help of a sharpened stick at the end of a string and a center pivot to draw the circle, as shown in figure 2. Divide and mark the perimeter of the circle at six roughly equal intervals.

Assembling the Poles

4. With a knife or hatchet, sharpen to a point the thicker ends of the six poles. Insert the sharpened ends of the poles 4" or more into the ground, placing them at your marks on the circle and angling them toward the center. Once you plant the trellis, the plants themselves will grow and help anchor the trellis more firmly to the ground.

5. Holding the tops of the poles together, bundle them together by wrapping 3' of tie wire three or four times around the

INSTRUCTIONS
Preparing the Ground

1. Lay out the materials in the gathering list on the ground, using figure 1 for reference. Our instructions will result in a trellis that's about 30" in diameter by roughly 6' tall. To make a smaller or

poles. Place the wire about 12" from the tops of the poles. Use a stepladder if necessary. Pull and tighten the wire with the pliers, then cut off any excess and tuck in loose ends.

Wrapping the Weavers

6. Decorate the top and hide the wire joint with a length of weaver loosely woven around the poles. Be sure to tuck in any stray ends of the weaver.

7. Complete the trellis by adding the bottom and middle weavers. Space them as suggested in figure 1, or make your own design. Starting at the bottom location 6" above the ground, use 1' of tie wire to secure the end of a weaver to one of the poles. Start wrapping the weaver around the posts in a loose spiral, weaving the vine in and out as you go. Add more weavers as needed, tucking in their ends, until you reach a width of 6" or so. Tuck in any final loose ends. Repeat in the same fashion for the middle weaver, but make this area 4" or so in width. Now let your new trellis watch over your bountiful harvest.

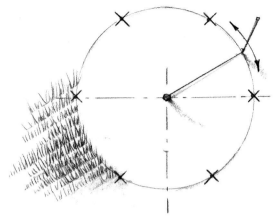

FIGURE 2: Layout Out Pole Locations

Variation

BAMBOO TIPI

Design by Will Hooker

Here's an easy-to-make support structure that's ideal for beans. It was made with Grey Henon Bamboo (Phyllostachys nigra 'Henon') but you can use any available bamboo. Since it isn't meant to last more than one season, you don't need to cure the bamboo; just use recently harvested poles. Follow the design principles for Down Home Pole Trellis, using wire instead of rubber bands. (Also see the bamboo projects on pages 121 and 123.) Cut 2½" to 3½"-diameter support poles, 11 to 12' long. Spiral wrap long bamboo splits around the poles, attaching them with nails or wire. Add something shiny at the top and plant the beans. In what seems like no time at all, the tipi will be covered with lovely green vines.

LOVING HEART TRELLIS

Adapted Design by Olivier Rollin

Even before roses climb to caress it, this trellis sends a heartfelt message. Wonderfully easy to make, it is really just a top and a bottom panel nailed together. Making it is a lovely way to learn how to bend and shape green wood.

WHAT YOU NEED
Basic Tool Kit
Rustic Tool Kit
Materials and Supplies
- $^3/_{32}$" drill bit for piloting 8d nails
- 2 pieces of $^1/_2$" rebar, 4' long
- 2 support blocks made of 2 x 4 scrap wood

Hardware
- 2 lbs. 8d common nails

GATHERING LIST

Code	Description	Qty.	Dimensions	Material
A	Uprights	5	1" diameter x 60" long	Green or dried
B	Crosspieces	6	1" diameter x 50" long	Green or dried
C	Heart Pieces	2	$^3/_4$" diameter x 30" long	Green
D	Fan Pieces	4	$^3/_4$" diameter x 30" long	Green or dried
E	Arch piece	1	$^3/_4$" diameter x 100" long	Green

Note: The lengths listed are approximate; you'll trim as you construct the trellis.

INSTRUCTIONS
Making the Rectangular Panel

1. The rectangular panel is 40" wide x 50" high, based on a gridwork of 10" x 10" squares. (See fig. 1.) With chalk, draw the grid on a flat work surface large enough for the layout, such as a sheet of plywood or a driveway.

2. Lay the five uprights (A) on the grid. Crosscut the center upright into two upper and lower sections, leaving approximately 1" of the lower section and 2" of the upper section extending beyond the horizontal grid lines, as shown in figure 1. The upper section of the center upright should extend 20" or so beyond the top of the grid. Extend the top ends of the remaining four uprights about 1" beyond the top of the grid. You'll trim the bottom ends later.

3. Position the six crosspieces (B) on top of the uprights. Cut the third crosspiece (as measured from the top of the grid) into two sections, and let each section extend about 1" past the middle uprights, as shown in figure 1.

4. Attach all the parts by drilling pilot holes and driving 8d nails at all the intersections. Drive the nails just enough to

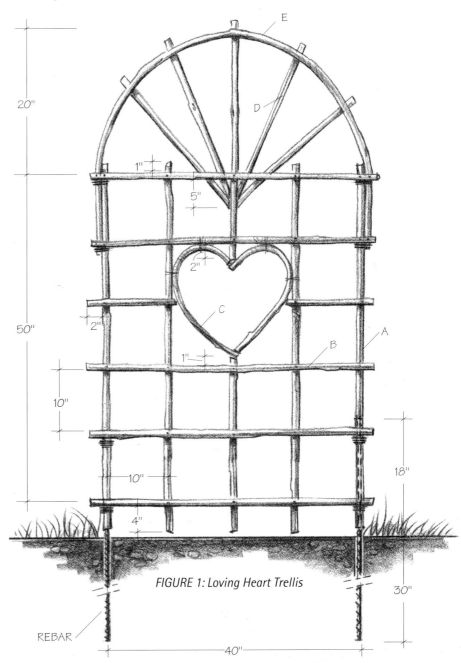

FIGURE 1: Loving Heart Trellis

The magenta-red Ernest Markham Clematis is a wonderful choice for beginning gardeners. It's a quick-climber and blooms profusely in the summer.

hold the pieces together, but stop short of driving the tips of the nails through the bottom pieces. Follow this procedure with all the subsequent nailing.

5. Shape the two heart pieces (C), trimming them with the loppers and nailing them to the protruding uprights and crosspieces. Drill pilot holes and secure the pieces with 8d nails. To reinforce the connection wrap tie wire where the heart touches the full-length uprights and crosspieces, as shown in figure 1.

6. Trim the crosspieces so they extend about 2" past the outer uprights; trim the upright ends about 4" from the bottom crosspiece.

Making the Arch

7. Position the fan pieces (D) on both sides of the center upright, about 5" below the top crosspiece. (See fig. 1.) Space the fan pieces evenly, and miter their ends with the loppers at an angle that fits them snugly against the upright. Drill pilot holes and secure them with 8d nails as you go, driving the nails through the fan pieces and into the top crosspiece and the center upright.

8. Measure up 20" from the center of the top crosspiece and mark the extended center upright and each fan piece.

9. Tie-wire one end of the arch piece (E) to one of the outer uprights at a point just below the second crosspiece. (See fig. 1.) Tie-wire the arch piece just below the top crosspiece.

10. Using the marks you made on the center upright and the fan pieces in step 8, make a free-form bend in the arch

piece. When you're satisfied with the curve, trim and tie-wire the free end to the opposite outer upright, using the same tie-wire technique as you did in step 9. Then drill pilot holes and drive an 8d nail into each intersection. Trim the ends of the fan pieces and the center upright 1" beyond the arch piece.

11. When all the joints have been nailed, transfer the trellis to scrap spacer blocks. Drive the nails all the way through the pieces so the heads are flush. (See how to nail several pieces together in the Traditional Fan Trellis project on page 39.) Once the nail heads are flush, turn the trellis over and bend all the protruding nail tips over with a hammer to stiffen all the joints.

Setting Up the Trellis

12. On the ground, mark where the two outer uprights meet the earth. Drive the two pieces of rebar about 30" into the ground at your marks, leaving roughly 18" above ground.

13. Position the trellis on the ground with its outer uprights aligned with the rebar. Tie-wire the rebar to the uprights just below the two lowest crosspieces, as shown in figure 1.

14. If the trellis is in an open area, you may need additional support to brace it against strong winds. Attach guide wires halfway up the sides of the trellis and tie the wires to stakes driven at an angle into the ground. When the trellis is in place, tie a ribbon on it and present it to your special someone.

DIAMOND PATTERN BAMBOO TRELLIS

Design by Anita Mattos

Give vegetable climbers, such as cucumbers, gourds, and tomatoes, a diamond-shaped bamboo trellis on which they can shine all season. Arrange several trellises to create a protective enclosure.

WHAT YOU NEED

Basic Tool Kit
Rustic Tool Kit
Additional Tools
  ↬ ³/₃₂" drill bit for piloting 1¼" and 2" screws
Materials and Supplies
  ↬ 2 pieces of ½" rebar, 4' long
Hardware
  ↬ ½ lb. 1¼" deck screws
  ↬ ½ lb. 2" deck screws

GATHERING LIST

2 posts of bamboo, 1 to 1¾" diameter x 4'

3 crosspieces of bamboo, 1 to 1¾" diameter x 7'

11 long diagonals of bamboo, ½ to 1" diameter x 6'

3 short diagonals of bamboo, ½ to 1" diameter x 4'

A bamboo trellis is sturdy enough to handle heavy vegetables, even these Whopper Cucumbers.

Cherry tomatoes look especially appealing when they're climbing on poles of bamboo.

Note: You'll need a fine-tooth saw, such as a conventional dovetail saw or a Japanese dovetail saw, for cutting bamboo because of its fibrous and splintery nature. If you want extra support for heavy vines, include a third post on the end of the trellis, as shown in the photograph.

INSTRUCTIONS

Cutting the Pieces

1. Cut all the pieces to length as shown in the gathering list.

Assembling the Pieces

2. Using the hammer, drive one of the rebar pieces into the bottom ends of the two posts to remove the inner node membrane from the lower 3' of the pole, creating a "sleeve."

3. On a large flat surface, lay out the posts 6' apart. Place the crosspieces on top, one 3" below the tops of the posts, one 3" above the bottom of the posts, and one equidistant between the other two. The crosspieces should extend about 6" past each post. Drill pilot holes at the intersections of the posts and crosspieces, and drive 2" screws.

Note: If you want a third post, add it at this time, locating it about 4" from the ends of the crosspieces, as shown in the photograph on page 121.

4. Mark the center of each crosspiece. You'll use these marks as reference points when placing the diagonals to form the diamond pattern.

5. Place five of the long diagonals and one of the short diagonals on the frame, all leaning in the same direction. Center the diagonals, drill pilot holes where the diagonals intersect the frame, and use the appropriate screws to secure the parts.

6. Turn over the trellis assembly. Lay out the remaining diagonal poles in the opposite direction to complete the diamond pattern. Adjust, drill pilot holes, and drive screws at all the intersections.

Installing the Trellis

7. Mark on the ground where the two end posts touch the earth. Pound the rebar into the ground at these points, leaving 12" to 18" above ground.

8. Call in your helper. Lift the trellis and slide the posts over the rebar.

9. Use tie wire to reinforce any intersections that need extra support. For a lovely, wild look, train your vines to crisscross on the diamond pattern.

ZIG-ZAG BAMBOO TRELLIS

Design by Carol Stangler

The zig-zag shapes of golden bamboo (phyllostachys aurea) shoot up like streaks of lightning in this dramatic trellis. Plant delicate vines to show off the striking design.

The Purple Hyacinth Bean is both lovely and delicious! Clusters of fragrant purple or white blooms are followed by pods bursting with sweet, edible peas.

WHAT YOU NEED

Basic Tool Kit
Rustic Tool Kit
Additional Tools
- ⅛" drill bit for piloting 2" screws
- Fine-tooth saw

Materials and Supplies
- 1 piece of ½" rebar, 5' long
- 2 bricks

Hardware
- ½ lb. 2" deck screws

Note: You'll need a fine-tooth saw, such as a conventional dovetail saw or a Japanese dovetail saw, for cutting bamboo because of its fibrous and splintery nature. If you don't have bamboo, you can modify the instructions and make the trellis from dry branches. Look for limbs that have interesting twists and turns.

GATHERING LIST

9 vertical uprights of zig-zag-shaped poles of golden bamboo, 1 to 1¾" in diameter, in lengths from 6' to 9'

3 crosspieces of zig-zag-shaped poles of golden bamboo, 1¼" in diameter, in lengths of 38", 54", and 62"

INSTRUCTIONS

Preparing the Center Pole

1. Select the longest and thickest of the nine vertical uprights to serve as the center pole, as shown in figure 1. Using the hammer, drive the rebar into the bottom end of the pole to remove the inner node membrane from the lower 3' of the pole, creating a "sleeve."

Weaving the Zig-Zag Design

2. On a driveway or other large, flat surface, lay out the vertical uprights in a fan shape with the zig-zag ends up. Start by placing the center pole in the middle and work outward, bringing the poles close together at the base, and fanning them out to 60" at the widest part. Position and adjust the poles to get a good fit.

3. One by one, lay out the horizontal crosspieces, weaving them over and under the uprights, as shown in figure 1. Work to create a surface with dimension.

4. When you're satisfied with your layout, use the saw to cut the poles to their finished lengths, as shown in figure 1.

Securing the Parts and Installing the Trellis

5. Where the vertical and horizontal poles intersect, drill pilot holes through the joints and secure them with 2" screws. Once you've driven screws through all the intersecting parts, turn over the structure and drill pilot holes and drive 2" screws again, from the other side into the intersections on the back side.

6. At your installation site, mark the ground for the center of the trellis and hammer in the rebar 18" to 24" deep. Place a brick on each side of the rebar, as shown in figure 1.

7. Hold the trellis over the rebar and slide the center pole over the rebar, resting the bottoms of the remaining poles on the bricks. If more stability is required, use tie wire and the appropriate fasteners to attach the trellis to the wall. Over a steaming cup of Chinese green tea, contemplate what other ordinary surfaces in your garden could be transformed with bamboo trellises.

The Chinese Trumpeter vine looks fantastic on bamboo. Hummingbirds love its peach summer bloom.

FIGURE 1:
Zig-Zag Bamboo Trellis

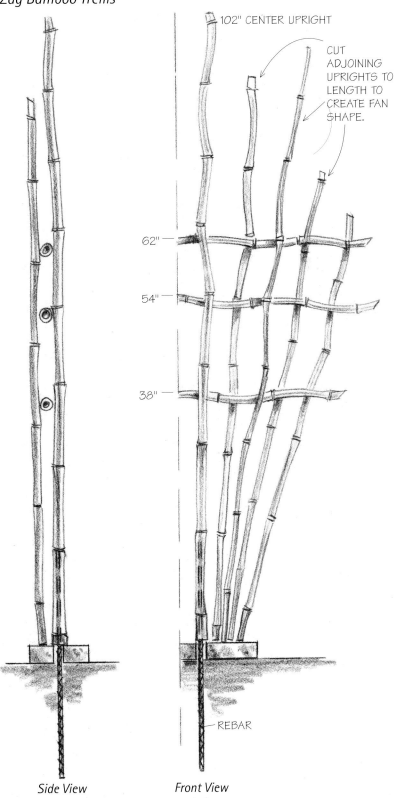

102" CENTER UPRIGHT

CUT ADJOINING UPRIGHTS TO LENGTH TO CREATE FAN SHAPE.

62"

54"

38"

REBAR

Side View   *Front View*

FOLDING SCREEN TRELLIS

Design by Kevin Barnes

With this convenient folding screen you can create privacy anywhere you want. When you're ready to receive company, just fold it out of the way. For a permanent look, surround the screen with pretty pots and train vines to climb it.

WHAT YOU NEED

Basic Tool Kit

Rustic Tool Kit

Materials and Supplies
- ↦ ⅙" drill bit for piloting 4d and 6d nails
- ↦ ³⁄₃₂" drill bit for piloting 8d nails
- ↦ 4 pieces of leather, 2 x 12", for hinges

Hardware
- ↦ 4d, 6d, 8d finish nails, as needed

INSTRUCTIONS

Cutting the Pieces

1. Cut the branches with the bowsaw. Keep in mind that the dimensions listed for the parts are approximate; don't worry if you cut them a little shorter or longer.

Building the Three Panels

2. Each panel consists of two uprights and four crosspieces. On a flat surface, work on one panel at a time, starting with two uprights and two crosspieces. Lay the two uprights about 16" apart, parallel to each other. Center the two crosspieces atop the uprights, roughly 6" in from each end of the uprights. Use a tape measure to read the diagonal measurements from opposite corners of the uprights, checking that the frame is square. When the two measurements are identical, drill pilot holes and drive 8d nails through the crosspieces and into the uprights. Repeat for the other two panels.

3. Turn the panels over so the crosspieces you attached in the previous step face down, then lay the panels side by side on your work surface. Arrange four filler pieces in each of the panels, laying each filler piece on top of the crosspieces. The bottom end of each filler piece should extend about 1" beyond the bottom crosspiece. Drill pilot holes and drive the

appropriate size nails through the filler pieces and into the crosspieces.

4. Without turning the panels over, position the remaining six crosspieces on top of the uprights, aligned with the crosspieces on the opposite side to sandwich the filler pieces. Drill pilot holes and use 8d nails to secure the crosspieces to the uprights.

Attaching the Hinges

5. Use the utility knife to cut the four strips of leather for the hinges. Starting with the middle panel, use two 4d nails to attach an end of one strip to one of the uprights about 6" below the top crosspiece. Attach the second strip to the opposite upright the same 6"-distance below the top crosspiece. Then nail the end of the third strip to the same upright, locating it 6" above the bottom crosspiece. Add the fourth strip to the opposite upright, 6" above the bottom crosspiece. Now wrap each strip of leather around the upright of the adjacent outer panel and position its free end over the corresponding nailed end on the upright of the middle panel. Use 4d nails to secure the end, taking care not to hit the nails already in place.

6. Stand the screen upright with the three panels in a zig-zag fashion to balance it. Pull up a chair and relax with a glass of lemonade and a good book.

6 uprights, 2" diameter, 6½' long, dried

12 crosspieces, 1" diameter, 18" long, dried

12 filler pieces with branches, ½ to 1" diameter, at least 6½" long

Peas on a porch? Sure! Plant a few vines of Sugar Lace peas in a planter and let them climb up your trellis.

The leather hinges are sturdy, yet allow the panels to be adjusted as needed.

FOUR-SEASON RUSTIC ARBOR

Adapted Design by Olivier Rollin

WHAT YOU NEED

Basic Tool Kit
Rustic Tool Kit
Digging Kit
Additional Tools
- $3/32$" drill bit for piloting $1\frac{1}{4}$" and 2"
- $1/8$" drill bit for piloting 3" screws
- $1/4$" drill bit
- 1" spade bit
- Circular saw (optional)

Materials and Supplies
- Post ground braces
- Pre-cut shims or thin strips of wood for shimming, as needed
- 2 pcs. 2 x 4 x 8', straight as possible

Hardware
- $1/2$ lb. 8d finish nails
- 1 lbs. $1\frac{1}{4}$" deck screws
- $1/2$ lb. 2" deck screws
- 1 lb. 3" deck screws
- 6 lag screws, 6" long, with washers

Big, bold, and beautiful in every season of the year, this monumental arbor puts on display the very essence of forest trees. If you're not lucky enough to find perfectly rounded limbs for the top, we explain how to create the arch with the pieces you do have. Plus we added lots of decorative loops just for the fun of it.

CUTTING LIST

Code	Description	Qty.	Dimensions	Material
A	Posts	8	4" to 5" in diameter, at least 10' long, as straight as possible	Dried
B	Crossbeams	2	5" in diameter, at least 70" long, straight as possible	Dried
C	Arch Pieces	4	4 to 5" in diameter, 5' long, with a natural curve	Dried
D	Angle Braces	4	4" in diameter, at least 16" long. Mitered at both ends	Dried
E	Side Beams	2	4 to 5" in diameter, at least 30" long	Dried
F	Roof Pieces	3	$3\frac{1}{2}$" in diameter, at least 30" long	Dried
G	Fan Pieces	14	$1\frac{1}{2}$" in diameter, at least 2' long, as straight as possible	Dried
H	Curved Fan Pieces	2	$1\frac{1}{2}$" in diameter, at least 72" long	Green
I	Side Lattice Pieces	28	branches $1\frac{1}{2}$ to 2" in diameter, 4' long	Green
J	Front and Back Lattice Pieces	24	$1\frac{1}{2}$ to 2" in diameter, at least 6" long	Dried

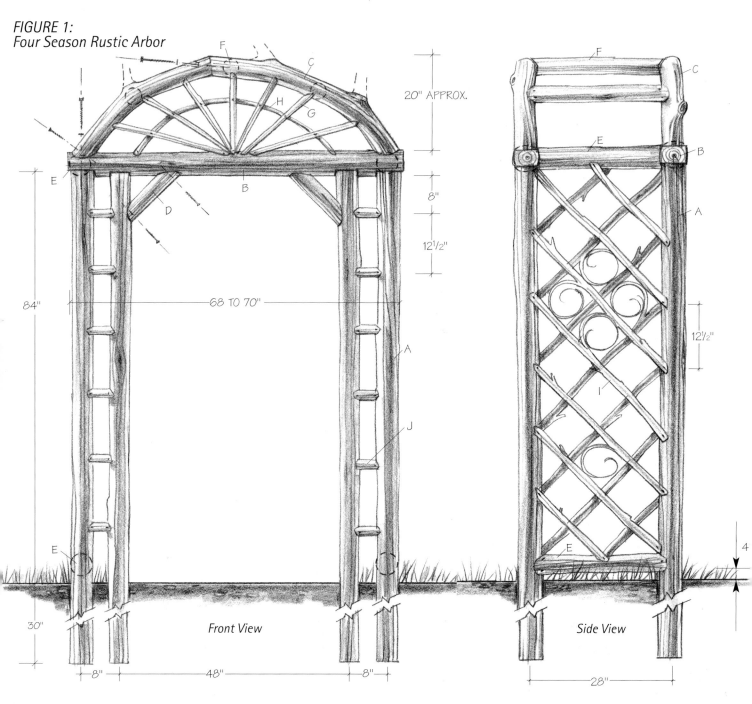

FIGURE 1:
Four Season Rustic Arbor

20" APPROX.

8"

12½"

84"

68 TO 70"

30"

Front View

8" — 48" — 8"

12½"

4

Side View

28"

INSTRUCTIONS
Preparing the Site and Digging Postholes

1. Dig four holes for the eight posts (A). See Preparing the Site (page 23) and Digging Postholes (page 26) and refer to project figures 1 and 2 for hole placement. Each pair of corner posts (A) will go into the same hole, which will also accommodate the space between the poles, so even though there are eight posts, you'll dig only four holes.

Cutting the Posts and Setting Them in the Ground

2. Cut the eight posts (A) to length as specified in the gathering list.

3. Call your helper. You'll start working with the front of the arbor first. With your helper on top of the stepladder to hold the posts, place one pair of posts into one of the front postholes. The posts should be 8" from each other, as measured from their centers, and roughly plumb. The tops of the posts don't need to be perfectly level with each other. Later, when you make the dado cuts on the crossbeam, you can make adjustments for any differences in post height.

4. Pack and tamp dirt around the posts firmly enough hold them upright so they don't fall, but not so tight that you can't move them. You'll have to adjust their positions slightly later.

5. Repeat steps 3 and 4 for the opposite pair of front posts.

Aligning the Posts

6. As shown in figure 2, use a straight 2 x 4 to help you align the centers of the four posts and to hold them in place. Using the dimensions in figure 2, mark the front of the 2 x 4 and drill pilot holes through each mark for 3" screws.

7. With your helper holding the 2 x 4 in place, drive 3" screws through the pilot holes and into the sides of the posts, as shown in figure 2. Don't drive the screws too tight. You'll have to make further adjustments in the next step.

8. To align the centers of the posts, drive a screw into the centerline on the tops of the two outer posts (it's okay to judge the centerlines by eye), then stretch a mason's line between the two screws,

as shown in figure 2. Nudge the inner posts under the string to align their centers with the outer posts. Now tighten all the screws holding the 2 x 4 to the posts. You may have to insert shims between a few posts and the 2 x 4 to keep them in alignment.

9. Repeat steps 3 through 8 to install the four posts for the back of the arbor, using a second 2 x 4 to hold this assembly in alignment.

10. See the information on temporary braces on page 28. Install post ground braces to the front posts, placing the bracing on the inside of the arbor to keep them out of the way.

Dadoing the Crossbeams

11. Work on one crossbeam (B) at a time, starting at the four front posts (A). Measure the now-fixed distance from the outer posts and cut a crossbeam to that length, or an inch or so longer. With

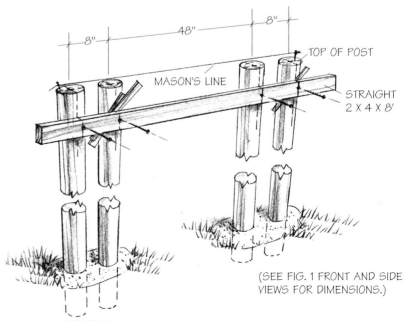

FIGURE 2: Aligning the Posts

your helper, place the crossbeam on top of the four posts, and center it so the ends extend evenly on both sides. Be sure to rotate the beam to find the best fit on top of the posts.

12. Working at the top of each post, draw chalk marks on the crossbeam for a dado. (Refer to page 19 for instructions on laying out and making dado cuts.)

13. Take the crossbeam down. Using the marks as a guide, cut the four dadoes 1" deep with the handsaw and chisel. Then reposition the crossbeam back on the posts and check the fit. Using the carpenter's level on the top of the crossbeam,

adjust the depth of the dado cuts if necessary with a chisel until the crossbeam sits level at the tops of the posts.

14. Once the crossbeam is leveled and fitted, take it down and set it on a flat work area with the dadoes facing sideways.

15. Repeat steps 11 through 14 to dado and fit the second crossbeam on the back side of the arbor.

Assembling the Arches

16. On your work area on the ground, arrange two arch pieces (C) above one of the crossbeams so they form a pleasing curve. The lower ends of the arch pieces should rest on top of the crossbeam at each end and the upper ends should overlap at the top. The curve should be approximately 20" high at its center and wide enough to span the width of the crossbeam, as shown in figure 1. Mark a vertical miter line on each of the arch pieces where they overlap at the top. Use the handsaw to cut the miters, and check that joint fits tightly. Don't cut the lower ends yet.

17. Clamp the arch miter joint to a piece of scrap plywood with C-clamps and use the 1" spade bit to drill an angled hole in the first piece, deep enough to countersink the head of the 6" lag screw. (See fig. 1.) Use the 1/4" bit to drill a pilot hole through the countersunk hole and into the second arch piece, deep enough to accommodate the length of the lag screw. Drive the lag screw through to secure the joint, and remove the C-clamps.

Golden is the word for this arbor in autumn, since it is covered with golden honeysuckle and the seedheads of the golden clematis that flowered in the summer.

18. In order to join the arch assembly to the crossbeam, you need to cut a bird's mouth joint on each end of the arch, as shown in figure 3. To cut the joint, position the arch assembly on top of the crossbeam, checking that the top of the arch is roughly 20" from the top of the crossbeam, with its lower ends overlapping the beam. Now mark where the ends of the arch meet the top of the crossbeam, and use a handsaw to cut the ends square to the marks.

19. Once you've cut the ends of the arch square, use the handsaw to cut 45∞ shoulders into each end of the arch, as shown in figure 3. Test the fit of the arch to the crossbeam, and make any necessary adjustments to the joint until the arch ends fit snugly over the beam.

20. Follow steps 16 through 19 to complete the second arch assembly.

Installing the Crossbeams and Arches

21. Lift one of the crossbeams (B) and reposition it on top of the appropriate set of posts. Drill a countersunk hole at each end of the beam with the 1" spade bit, centered over the ends of the outer posts. (See fig. 1.) Then use the ¼" bit to drill pilot holes through the ends of the beam and into the posts, and drive the lag screws to secure the beam to the outer posts.

22. Drill angled pilot holes on both sides of the crossbeam and toenail two 3" screws through the beam and into each inner post. Remove the 2 x 4, and repack and tamp the dirt firmly around the postholes.

23. Repeat steps 21 through 22 to secure the second crossbeam.

24. Find your helper. Retrieve one of the arch assemblies and position it on top of the corresponding crossbeam. Drill pilot holes through the ends of the arch and secure it to the crossbeam with four 3" screws at each end. (See fig. 1.)

25. Repeat step 24 to install the second arch.

Cutting and Attaching the Angle Braces

26. There are two steps involved in cutting the four angle braces (D), both using the handsaw. First, make a 45° miter cut on each end of the braces, such that the braces measure 16" from long point to long point. Check the fit of the braces to the posts, and make any necessary adjustments until the miters sit squarely on the posts. With the miters cut, the second step is to cut the bird's mouth on each end of each brace, as shown in figure 3.

27. With your helper holding each brace in position against an inner post and the underside of the crossbeam, drill pilot holes through the ends of the braces and install them with 3" screws.

Installing the Side Beams

28. It's time to install the four side beams (E) at the top and bottom sides of the arbor, as shown in figure 1. Working at one of the bottom locations, measure

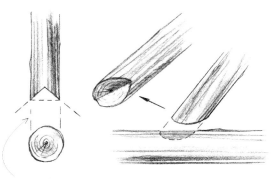

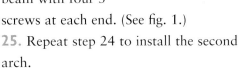
CUT 45° SHOULDERS ON BOTH SIDES OF LIMB WITH HANDSAW.

FIGURE 3: Bird's Mouth Joint

the distance between two outer posts, and cut a side beam a few inches longer than this measurement with the handsaw, making sure the ends are square. With some trial and error, you can achieve a good fit of the beam between the posts using the following technique:

29. Cut a bird's mouth in one end of the beam with a handsaw (see fig. 3), then hold the beam up to the posts. Using your eye to gauge how much material you need to remove from the square end of the beam, make a second square cut on that end, then cut the second bird's mouth. Insert the beam by angling it into the space between the posts, and tapping it level with a hammer or small sledgehammer. Once the side beam is in position, drill pilot holes through the ends of the beam and secure it to the posts with four 3" screws at each end. Repeat this test-fitting and cutting procedure to install the remaining side piece at the opposite bottom side, and to install the two side beams at the top of the arbor.

Installing the Roof Pieces

30. The three roof pieces (F) connect the two arches at the top of the arbor. To fit and install the roof pieces, use the same procedure as you did to install the side beams. Cut each roof piece slightly longer than necessary, then cut a bird's mouth in one end and gauge the fit of the piece to the arches. Re-cut the square end to length, and cut the bird's mouth on that end, too. Drill pilot holes and install the roof pieces onto the arch with 3" screws.

Installing the Fan Pieces

31. To complete the two arches, install the fan pieces (F) as shown in figure 1. Place each fan piece in position and mark where the piece overlaps the arch and crossbeam. Cut the miters to your marks with a handsaw. Once you've fit the fan pieces, drill angled pilot holes in their ends and install them to the arch and crossbeam with 2" screws.

Attaching the Curved Fan Pieces

32. Mark the back side of the fan pieces you just installed on both arches, making pencil or chalk marks roughly in the centers of the fans to help in positioning the curved fan pieces (H). Working on one arch at a time, hold a curved fan piece behind the fan pieces, and bend it to your marks. Use C-clamps to help with positioning the piece. Once you have a pleasing curve, mark and cut the ends of the curved fan piece with the bowsaw so they're flush with the crossbeam. Drill pilot holes and drive 8d finish nails through the curved fan piece and into the fan pieces and the top of the crossbeam. Repeat for the second curved fan piece. Remove the clamps.

Installing the Lattice

33. Refer to figure 1 to see the layout of the side lattice pieces (I), made from green stock. The pieces cross one another in their centers and are attached at roughly a 45° angle onto the posts. Mark the centers of the side beams (E) and mark both sides of the posts every 12½" where the lattice pieces will be attached.

Note: To lay out the first 12½" mark at the tops of the posts, hold a piece of lattice stock in the center of the upper side beam and angle it down approximately 45° on both posts.

34. Starting at the top of the arbor, trim each end of a side lattice piece with the loppers, cutting a miter so the end butts against the curve of the posts. Fit the first piece with one mitered end on your center mark on the upper side beam, and its lower end on the first mark on the corresponding post. Drill pilot holes, and attach the lattice piece to the beam and the post with 1¼" screws driven through the miters.

35. Attach the remaining lattice pieces on both sides of the arbor. You'll need to alternate between the inside and the outside of the posts as you fit and attach the lattice pieces, as shown in figure 1. Where the lattice pieces intersect, drill pilot holes and secure these joints with 2" screws.

Note: To make the decorative loops shown in figure 1, you'll need to first create the loops on the lattice pieces before attaching them. Using a sharp knife or the hatchet, slice a strip about 20" long on each lattice piece, keeping one end of the strip attached to the piece. Then secure the lattice piece to the arbor and gently shape the strip into a loop between lattice pieces. If necessary, secure the loop to the surrounding lattice pieces with tie wire.

34. Refer to figure 1 for the layout of the front and back lattice pieces (J). You can use the same marks you made on the posts in step 32 to locate these pieces. As you did with the side lattice pieces, miter the ends of the front and back lattice pieces, this time using a handsaw since the stock is dry. Miter the pieces so their ends fit snugly between the posts, then drill pilot holes and secure the pieces to the posts with 1¼" screws. Now get ready to enjoy your arbor in the ever-changing seasons to come.

The arbor is naturally adorned for the winter holidays by the golden clematis seedheads still clinging to it.

RUGGED LOG ARBOR

Design by Joel Cole

WHAT YOU NEED

Rustic Tool Kit
Digging Kit
Additional Tools
- ⅛" drill bit for piloting 3" screws
- Chainsaw (optional)

Materials and Supplies
- Ground post braces

Hardware
- 1 lb. 3" deck screws

Large limbs—which are practically logs—add a primitive heft to this solid, foursquare arbor. Allow a medley of plants to claim the arbor as their own to keep the wild look all year long.

GATHERING LIST

Code	Description	Qty.	Dimension	Material
A	Posts	4	5 to 6" diameter x 120"	Green or dried
B	Crossbeams	4	3½ to 4" diameter x 66"	Green or dried
C	Top Beams	4	3 to 3½" diameter x 66"	Green or dried
D	Side Rails	4	3 to 3½" diameter x 58"	Green or dried
E	Panel Pieces	12	1½ to 2" diameter x 54"	Green

INSTRUCTIONS

Cutting the Parts

1. Cut all the parts to the lengths listed, using a handsaw (for dry stock), bowsaw (for green stock), or chainsaw. You can use green or dried stock for all the parts, except for the panel pieces (E), which should be green so they're pliable enough for weaving together later.

Digging the Holes and Installing the Posts

2. Call in your helpers. See Preparing the Site (page 23) and Digging Postholes (page 26), and refer to project figure 1 for dimensions. Dig the holes for the posts.

3. Once the holes are dug, position the posts (A) in the holes, making sure they're plumb. Brace the posts securely. Don't worry if the tops of the posts aren't precisely level with each other, since any slight inconsistencies only add to the charm of this rustic project.

Adding the Roof

4. With your helpers and a stepladder or two, attach the first lower crossbeam (B) to one side of the arbor, locating it on the inside of the two corresponding posts. First mark 6" down from the tops of the four posts, then lift up the cross-

FIGURE 1: Log Arbor

beam to a pair of marks. The ends of the beam should extend about 6" beyond the posts. While holding the beam on your marks, drill angled pilot holes and toenail two 3" screws through the underside of the beam and into each post. Repeat to install the second lower crossbeam on the opposite side, then stiffen the connections by wrapping each joint with 4' strips of tie wire. Be sure to wrap the wire around each crossbeam as well as over and under the adjoining post. Pull the wire tight with pliers to ensure a strong joint.

5. Add the two remaining upper crossbeams (B) on top of the lower crossbeams, orienting them across the front and back of the arbor, as shown in figure 1. Center the beams over the outsides of the posts, with their ends extending roughly 6" past the posts. Drill pilot holes and secure the beams by toenailing

3" screws through the beams and into the posts and the lower crossbeams.

6. Lay the four top beams (C) on top of the two lower crossbeams (B), centering the top beams so their ends extend about 6" beyond the lower crossbeams. Space the top beams evenly between he upper crossbeams. Drill angled pilot holes and toenail 3" screws through the top beams and into the lower crossbeams.

Installing the Sides

7. Attach the four side rails (D) to each side of the arbor, as shown in figure 1. Measuring from the ground up, make a mark on the insides of all four posts at 18" and 72", respectively. (See fig. 1.) Working on one side of the arbor, have your helper assist you in holding a side rail against the lower pair of marks on the posts. Drill angled pilot holes and toenail a pair of 3" screws through each end of the rail and into the posts. Repeat for the upper rail on the same side of the arbor, holding that rail on your 72" marks. Use the same procedure to install the lower and upper rails on the opposite side of the arbor.

8. Working on one side of the arbor, weave six panel pieces (E) in a crisscross fashion on the inside of the arbor, as shown in figure 1. Drill pilot holes through the ends of the panel pieces and secure them to the posts and the side rails with 3" screws. To strengthen the panels, drill pilot holes and drive 3" screws into the joints where the panel pieces intersect. Repeat to complete the other side of the arbor. Use sturdy hanging hooks to display flowerpots or wind chimes from the arbor roof—they'll look wonderful.

GROWING GRAPES

The grape was one of the first plants ever cultivated, about 30,000 years ago in the Middle East. Though the vines grew naturally along the ground, Neolithic gardeners eager for the juice of the grape soon trained grapevines to grow up poles. The addition of a crossbar atop two forked poles proved to be the perfect arrangement for growing grapes—and the modern arbor was born.

You don't need as much space as a vineyard to grow your own grapes. A garden-size, but sturdy, arbor should do just fine. The whole project of the grape arbor can be a family project: finding out what types of grapes grow best in your region (you'd be surprised how many varieties of grapes you can choose from!), planting in the early spring, pruning during the rapid growth in the summer, picking the fruit in the

Green-gold Niagara grapes are sweet and juicy. Once established, the vines need only occasional watering.

autumn, and letting the vines go dormant in the winter.

Grapes need full sun and high temperatures to ripen fully, so place your arbor accordingly. Plant the vines in well-drained soil in holes large enough for the roots to spread out, but not too deep. Prune the vines back to two buds when planting, and as the vine grows, select the strongest cane and train it up the arbor post.

If you don't want to prune the vines, let them grow naturally. You'll have fewer grapes in exchange for a dense, shady roof overhead.

VISIONARY ARBOR

Design by J. Dabney Peeples

WHAT YOU NEED
Basic Tool Kit
Rustic Tool Kit
Digging Kit
Materials and Supplies
- ⚬ $\frac{1}{16}$" drill bit for piloting 6d nails
- ⚬ $\frac{3}{32}$" drill bit for piloting 8d nails
- ⚬ $\frac{1}{8}$" drill bits for piloting 10d nails
- ⚬ Brick, or other heavy object
- ⚬ 4 pieces of $\frac{1}{2}$" rebar, 4' long

Hardware
- ⚬ 1 lb. assorted finish nails (in sizes from 6d to 10d)

GATHERING LIST

4 uprights, $2\frac{1}{2}$" diameter x 8', dried

14 crosspieces, 1 to $1\frac{1}{2}$" diameter x 2', dried

2 crossbeams, 1 to $1\frac{1}{2}$" diameter x 2' to 3', dried

Assorted smaller-diameter branches for filler, dried

Note: You can substitute other branches for the rhododendron if you wish, and plant the vine of your choice to cover the arbor.

INSTRUCTIONS
Gathering and Cutting the Pieces

1. Gather your materials, looking for four dried, naturally curved limbs for the uprights. To help gauge how much curve you need for each upright, plan on an archway about 4' wide when each pair of uprights is placed side by side. Use the handsaw to cut the branches to the lengths required.

Building the Sides of the Arbor

2. Select a flat work surface, such as a picnic table or a sheet of plywood laid across sawhorses. You'll work on one side of the arbor at a time. Lay two uprights on the work surface, parallel to each other and roughly 2' apart, with the larger-diameter bottom ends on the work surface. Let the unsupported ends of the uprights hang off the work surface if necessary, so the area you're working on is stable and lies relatively flat. Make sure the curves are oriented in the same direction.

3. Starting about 4" from the bottoms of the uprights, measure and mark 16" intervals along both uprights. Center a crosspiece atop the two uprights on the lowest marks. Drill pilot holes and secure the crosspiece to the uprights with

You need vision to create this arbor, for it can take several years for the growing vines to achieve their magical look. Made of sturdy rhododendron branches, this "natural" arbor shimmers with the silvery leaves of an elaeagnus shrub trained to climb over it.

The Happy Wanderer is a blooming oddball. Its pretty drooping clusters of violet flowers show off in late winter and early spring.

nails, choosing a nail length that penetrates both pieces without going all the way through. Use a brick if necessary to help hold the pieces in place and to provide resistance to the force of your hammer blows. If you're not used to nailing thick, flexible wood, ask your helper to help you hold the branches while you nail them. If a nail does pierce both branches, bend the protruding tip with the hammer. Continue in this fashion to attach the remaining six crosspieces along the pair of uprights, positioning each crosspiece on the next set of 16" marks and nailing it to the uprights to form a ladder-like structure. Attach the last crosspiece at the very top ends of the uprights.

4. Repeat steps 2 and 3 to build the other side of the arbor.

Attaching the Sides and the Crossbeams

5. With your helper, place the two finished side assemblies on their sides, so the tops of the uprights and the uppermost crosspieces touch and the bottom ends are spread about 4' apart. Use three 3' strips of tie wire to bind the tops of the sides together, wrapping one strip around the adjoining crosspieces in the middle and the other two strips at the arbor's outer edges. As you wrap each outer edge, be sure to weave the wire around the crosspieces and over and under the uprights.

6. Use the two crossbeams to help tie the top of the structure together. Working on the side of the arbor that's facing up, measure 16" from the top and

mark the two uprights. Center a crossbeam on your marks, drill pilot holes where the beam overlaps the uprights, and secure the beam to the uprights with nails. If the beam extends more than a few inches past the uprights, trim off the excess with a handsaw. Carefully turn the arbor over, and repeat to attach the second crossbeam to the opposite side.

Adding the Filler Pieces

7. With the aid of your helper, stand the arbor upright and nail the filler branches to the uprights and the crosspieces, filling in the sides and top. If you place these smaller branches creatively with their ends touching the ground, you can make it look as though the arbor grew where it will stand. Drill pilot holes and be careful to choose the appropriate-length nails when attaching these pieces.

Positioning the Arbor

8. Clear your chosen site and rake it free of debris. (See Preparing the Site on page 23.)

9. Have your helper assist you in placing the arbor on your site. To stabilize and secure the arbor, drive the four pieces of rebar into the ground adjacent to where the uprights touch the ground. Use a heavy hammer or sledge to pound the rebar into the ground, leaving 12" to 18" above ground. Then use tie wire to attach the uprights to the rebar to complete the project. Now plant your vines at the base of the arbor and wait for the magic to start.

Acknowledgments

Helpers are beneficial when making arbors and trellises–they are absolutely essential in making a book. We were lucky to have them in abundance:

Technical Editor ANDY RAE, master woodworker and wordsmith, who hammered, cut, glued, drilled, polished, and smoothed our rough ideas into a real book

Art Director CELIA NARANJO, who showered the book design with her usual flair, and art department intern SHANNON NELSON whose help was invaluable

Assistant Editor VERONIKA ALICE GUNTER, whose sunny enthusiasm warmed every stage of the book; proofreader DIANE WEINER from whom no errant comma dare hide; the editorial assistance team of RAIN NEWCOMB, DANA LADE, ANNE WOLFF HOLLYFIELD, and NATHALIE MORNU, who valiantly dug deep for research yet kept us on solid ground throughout; and production assistants HANNES CHAREN and MEGAN KIRBY, who prove the joy of teamwork

Deep appreciation goes to each of the following:

For the generous use of their photographs
JACKSON & PERKINS, (800) 292-4769, www.jacksonandperkins.com, rose photos on pp. 33 (Cecile Brunner climbing rose) and 93 (Dream Weaver rose)

MONROVIA GROWERS, (888-Plant It), www.monrovia.com, rose and flower photos on pp. 32, 33 (excluding top right hand photo), 51, 64, 77, 87, 90, 93 (white Banksian rose), 98, 104, 110, 120, 139, and 142

PARK SEED COMPANY, (800) 845-3369, www.parkseed.com, vegetable photos on pp. 122, 124, and 127

ROBERT E. LYONS, PH.D., Director, J.C. Raulston Arboretum, North Carolina State University, Raleigh, NC, p. 117

THOMAS G. RANNEY, PH.D., Professor of Horticultural Science, North Carolina State University, Fletcher, NC, p. 125

For their technical expertise
THOMAS STENDER, www.stenderdesign.com

OTTO ZAHN, Woodworking Instructor, Edwards Air Force Base, CA

For their horticultural advice
WOMEN'S GARDEN CLUB of Asheville, NC, Evelyn Wyatt, President

PEGGY PINEAU, Nova Scotia, Canada, heirloom rose gardener, www.oldheirloomroses.com

TIM RITZ, Ritler Ridge Vineyards, Candler, NC, (828) 665-7405

Contributing Designers

ANTIQUE ROSE EMPORIUM in central Texas is a garden and mail order company devoted to the character and charm of old garden roses. They design and embellish many different structures to show off their roses, (800) 441-0002, www.weareroses.com.

KEVIN BARNES of Asheville, NC, builds rustic indoor and outdoor furniture and art pieces and creates outdoor sanctuary spaces, (828) 232-0953, kpaulbarnes@aol.com.

JOEL COLE of Weaverville, NC, is an avid gardener and artist who draws most of the inspiration for his creative endeavors from his garden, (828) 658-3057, joelcole@juno.com.

WILL HOOKER, Ph.D. is a bamboo artist and Professor of Landscape Horticulture, North Carolina State University, Raleigh, NC, Will_Hooker@ncsu.edu.

ANITA MATTOS is a master gardener and horticulturalist who lives in Puerto Rico.

J. DABNEY PEEPLES DESIGN ASSOCIATES, INC. of Easley, SC, is one of the leading landscape design firms in the southeastern U.S. and a frequent contributor to Lark Books, (864) 859-6570.

CAROL STANGLER, bamboo artist in Asheville, NC, is the author of *The Craft & Art of Bamboo*, (Lark Books 2001). She can be reached at Bird Tribe Studio, 828-254-0023, CStangler@aol.com.

MARK STROM is a well-known woodworker, sculptor, and artist in Asheville, NC, (828) 258-1445.

JANE WILSON is an artist/designer/gardener in Black Mountain, NC, who comes from an Appalachian family who made every item they used. Her specialty is sewing arts, especially architectural wall tapestries. (828) 280-1782

Metric Conversion Table

INCHES	CENTIMETERS
⅛	3 mm
¼	6 mm
⅜	9 mm
½	1.3
⅝	1.6
¾	1.9
⅞	2.2
1	2.5
1¼	3.1
1½	3.8
1¾	4.4
2	5
2½	6.25
3	7.5
3½	8.8
4	10
4½	11.3
5	12.5
5½	13.8
6	15
7	17.5
8	20
9	22.5
10	25
11	27.5
12	30
13	32.5
14	35
15	37.5
16	40
17	42.5
18	45
19	47.5
20	50
21	52.5
22	55
23	57.5
24	60
25	62.5
26	65
27	67.5
28	70
29	72.5
30	75
31	77.5
32	80
33	82.5
34	85
35	87.5
36	90

Index